ALONG THE
AFRIC SHORE

RUSSELL WARREN HOWE

ALONG THE
AFRIC SHORE

An historic review of two centuries
of U.S.–African relations

BARNES & NOBLE
BOOKS
10 East 53d St., New York 10022
(a division of Harper & Row Publishers, Inc.)

© Russell Warren Howe, 1975

First Edition, 1975

Published in the U.S.A. 1975 by
HARPER & ROW PUBLISHERS, INC.
BARNES & NOBLE IMPORT DIVISION

ISBN 0 06 493021 1

Printed in Great Britain by
Cox & Wyman Ltd,
London, Fakenham and Reading

To my children

Author's Note

My first intention was to combine a review of diplomatic relations with Africa with a full study of contemporary U.S. policy toward Africa and the conflicting critiques of this, including my own. It soon became clear that two different books would be required. This book is simply a history. A study of contemporary policy will follow later.

This survey is far from exhaustive; nor is it a diplomatic history in the formal sense. I have exercised the newsman's prerogative to select and emphasize what I have felt is significant and to eschew a great deal of detail. This was made easier by the fact that, for much of the period under review, there was no coherent policy as such to trace. In the modern era, when policies began to emerge, contraction was essential to avoid over-emphasis on events that might lose significance with perspective.

Acknowledgement of some of the helpful cooperation which I received is mentioned in the source appendix. Particular gratitude is expressed to Ambassador William Hall, then Director-General of the Foreign Service, for his assistance with tracking down illustrations. I should also like to express my thanks to the present and former director and staff of the Woodrow Wilson International Center for Scholars at the Smithsonian, where I began and completed this book during two periods as a Guest Scholar.

R.W.H.

Contents

I

II

Illustrations

Appearing between pages 86–7

1. Seal Page, United States–Morocco Friendship Treaty, 1786, signed by John Adams and Thomas Jefferson. Oldest US treaty still in force.
   Ceremonial letter from the King of Morocco acknowledging the Instruments of Ratification of the 1786 Treaty by the Continental Congress.

2. Ratification Instruments of the 1840 Treaty with Zanzibar.
   Ceremonial letter from Premier Rainilaiarivony of Madagascar to Consul Waller, 1858.

3. Seal pages of the 1905 Treaty with Emperor Menelik of Ethiopia in Amharic, French and English, signed by President Theodore Roosevelt.

4. The first American Embassy in Africa: the Monrovia Legation building, *circa* 1880.

5. U.S. Delegates to the Berlin Conference, 1884–85
   John Adams Kasson
   Henry Shelton Sanford
   Henry Morton Stanley

6. Consul Skinner's Mission to Addis Ababa
   The party in front of its mansion
   The party leaving the audience chamber

7. Figures in the Ethiopian Drama
   Hofmann Philip
   Cornelius van H. Engert
   Cordell Hull
   Wallace Murray
   Emperor Haile Selassie and President Franklin D. Roosevelt

8. World War Two Diplomats
   Clifton Wharton
   Felix Cole
   Clare Timberlake
   Henry Serrano Villard

Envoys to the Congo
Edmund Gullion
Sheldon Vance
Authors of Reports
Julius Holmes
Edward Korry
Charles Darlington

I

PART ONE
1776–1884
The Age of Outposts

The Ethiope Factor in Foreign Policy

Africa's impact on the United States in this generation – at all costs, when seen from a State Department point of view – has seemed to make itself felt with colorful suddenness. The emergence of the black continent caught policymakers by surprise. Awareness that this emergence had caught Africans by surprise as well only gave the situation a surrealistic flavor.

The African revolution to which the then Senator Kennedy referred in 1958 coincided with a black revolution in the United States, largely set in motion by the Supreme Court's school desegregation order of 1954. The African revolution fueled and exemplified the civil rights conflict in America, tinging it with an idealistic streak of Afro-Zionism that reversed a century of traditional Negro contempt for Africa: this zionism, in turn, spawned a trend of black segregationism – which partially respectabilized traditional white separatism.

'Color-conscious' because of its domestic problems, the Establishment in Washington tended to look at Africa, not coldly and pragmatically as just another Third World zone, but as a vast region where America had a special responsibility. It was clear, from the start, that Americans felt more empathy or sympathy for Africa than they felt for Latin America or for Asia. Emotion, paternalism, ultra-sensitivity on both sides of the Middle Atlantic often vitiated judgment

3

in Washington and produced a genuine human dilemma in policymaking which still persists. Early misconceptions on both sides led to early disappointments. The darkly beautiful bartered bride of the late Fifties, treating East and West with promiscuous evenhandedness, took on the policymaker's image of a painted harridan ten years later.

Noone has a right to be surprised. Once Caliban was identified – as the inadequate creature whom the Prosperos of imperialism had unleashed on the unsuspecting modern world –could Sycorax be far behind? Almost inevitably, there was a search for a new inscrutability, which would serve as a pretext for the storm in African relations. These, it was now explained, were a novelty that was still poorly understood. Yet in fact African–American diplomacy is not as new a factor on the political-history landscape as might be thought. It goes back to the days of the Philadelphia Congress. Indeed, few areas of the world have been so consistently host to such a large number of those Americans whose task, as Lord Acton said of diplomats, is to lie abroad for their native land.

Consuls in Barbary

The first Continental Congress of the United States regarded a diplomatic budget much as a Vermont storekeeper would look on a budget for advertising. The Congress was only half-convinced of its necessity, and wary of how far downhill such a slippery spending path might lead. The fathers of the nation saw diplomats as effete, as part of a tradition which America was busy rejecting: diplomats were persons who lived abroad by choice and according to the manners of Europe. When war broke out with Algiers in 1812, the budget of the United States for 'foreign intercourse' throughout the world was sixty thousand dollars – less than four per cent of the ransom money for prisoners eventually paid to the troublesome *Dey* in order to end the conflict.

Yet the United States was the Bangladesh of its day and

needed foreign wellwishers badly, to counterbalance at least one major foreign power that sought to destroy its independence. The United States also had commercial relations to defend: late eighteenth-century America was far from the self-sufficiency it attained about a century later. It needed raw materials for some of its infant industries, and most of these came from the tropical world. United States relations with black Africa in the first decade or so of the Republic's independence were conditioned by trade.

After the French Revolution of 1789, however, the embroilment of Europe in a quarter-century of quasi-permanent warfare gave strategic as well as purely commercial significance to Mediterranean Africa, because of the need to ensure safeconduct for American shipping and supplies. Consulates were maintained at Cairo, Tripoli, Tunis, Algiers and especially at Tangier and Gibraltar. These 'protected' the Straits that were Europe's main corridor to the Atlantic at a time when northern European ports were engulfed in conflict.

One of America's earliest treaties with a foreign power – the oldest still valid today – was with the King of Morocco, Sidi Mohammed, in 1786. There is some scholarly doubt concerning the dates on which the protocols were signed, but those usually given are June 28 and July 15, 1786. The treaty was sealed at Marrakesh by a Special Agent, Thomas Barclay, in behalf of Envoys Plenipotentiary John Adams (Minister in London), Thomas Jefferson (Paris) and Benjamin Franklin. It contained the usual terms of a military alliance and obligated Morocco to treat the United States commercially on the same basis as it treated Spain – what is invariably referred to, now, as mostfavored-nation treatment. U.S. consuls were to reside in 'any Sea Port of our Dominions that they shall think proper'. This meant Tangier.

Similar treaties were signed with the Turkish *Dey* of Algiers in 1795, with the '*Bey* and Subjects of Tripoli of Barbary' the following year and with the *Bey* of Tunis a year later. Tripolitania, Tunisia and Algeria were under the decaying writ of the Ottoman empire. Morocco was independent – hence its priority position in treaties meant to solve the corsair question.

The day was May 30, 1793. The warmth of the clear, Tangerine sun was tempered by a damp squall which gingered

5

the whitecaps in the Straits and prised at the hastily furled sails of the *Rosita* as it swung around on the rudder by the Ishak Lufti landing in Tangier harbor. A boatswain lassooed a capstan and shouted through brown broken teeth to the Berber boatman stern-oaring up to take the other cable.

Consul James Simpson of Massachusetts was on the landing. He had only been *en poste* for six weeks and was impatient for his first pouch from Philadelphia. A gangplank with a carved balister was pushed oversides and lashed to the timber taffrail. The Portuguese captain came ashore, followed by his mate with the ship's papers. The captain himself carried the leather pouch with the new symbol of the eagle, tied with silk cord, carefully sealed with crimson wax. Simpson seemed relieved to get it, even though it dealt mostly with budgetary strictures on his new mission.

Consul Simpson, a spare man with ruddy curls and an earnest manner that contrasted with the air of studied indifference that characterized most of his colleagues, put the pouch in his redingote, worming it down behind the belt. He remounted his pony, which carried him slowly up the steep hill of the Casbah, back to Simpson's small drab villa. By afternoon, he was already responding, anxious to catch the brigantine before it weighed anchor on the dawn tide for Baltimore the following day. His quill recorded faithfully the movements past Gibraltar of the great powers' fleets since he arrived.

America's main African mission, then, was at Tangier, where the consulate was occupied by Simpson from April 20, 1793 to January 1, 1803. His despatches were sent to Philadelphia or to David Humphreys, the Revolution colonel who was minister to Portugal. The King, referred to in correspondence at the time as the Emperor, was in residence at Mogador (modern Essouira) except in the hot season, when he rode to Rabat.

Simpson shared the Tangier post with consuls from England, France, the Netherlands, Denmark, Sweden, Portugal, Genoa and Spain. The Genoese agent initially represented Ragusa and Venice also. Relations with the great powers, especially England which still regarded him as a rebellious British citizen, were tenuous, and Simpson was as prickly as modern-day Irish

6

diplomats. Simpson had closer relations with the Scandinavian consuls, and with the Portuguese, and usually used Portuguese brigantines to carry his despatches to America.

From Barclay, he inherited three local contacts: Giuseppe Chiappe, a local trader, Chiappe's brother in Mogador, and Mulay (Prince) Saib in Fez – later superseded by Prince Othman, until Othman died in the plague epidemic of 1801–2. These men were not only informers, but lobbyists who influenced the court in favor of the new republic across the seas, and passed on the meager gifts approved by Congress – '*car tout ici se fait par interêt*', as Giuseppe Chiappe remarks in an early missive to Simpson requesting a long overdue payment to himself. Chiappe, who apparently already knew how irregular new nations could be on bills, was not above writing direct to George Washington for his money.

Fulfilling its part of the treaty, the U.S. gave, in 1798, bolts of muslin, damask and Holland cloth, along with tea, sugar and English candy – which was such a success that Simpson had to send to London for more. In comparison, the more affluent Portuguese presented sixty mules and fifty camels. The Danes gave twentyfive thousand dollars in specie. But there is a modern touch in Simpson's relieved report to Secretary of State Timothy Pickering that 'I am happy to tell you there was not a Syllable said [by the Emperor] on the subject of [any request for] Military Stores'.

Simpson's problems were usually more financial than political, and some of his political problems might have been avoidable if he had had a larger bribe budget and had cut less of a modest figure. He was paid two thousand dollars a year (twice as much as most United States consuls in Europe at the time), compared to the four thousand dollars of the Scandinavians, the twenty thousand livres of the French and the twelve hundred sovereigns of the British consul. He was invariably in debt, awaiting salary: he borrowed from colleagues or simply wrote drafts on the Secretary of State. He tried in vain to get his stipend doubled, even offering to occupy both the Gibraltar and Tangier posts as 'Consul in Barbary'. His first house, he noted, was 'unfit for any Christian to be in, far less . . . the Consul of the United States'. He pleaded in vain for $2,136 to buy a 'decent' house which he had found. For years, he continued to write proudly (in triplicate, for

7

security, sent in three different ships) from 'Mount Washington, near Tangier'; but even this courtesanship was to no avail.

At Gibraltar and Tangier the consulates kept watch, as best they could, on the English squadron in the Straits and off Cadiz, along with naval movements generally. On February 10, 1799, for instance, Consul Simpson informed Philadelphia that the '*ci-devant* Venetian Fleet passed to the Westward in the night of the 7th instant.' This despatch and its information would have reached the Department of State more than two weeks later.

The Berber emperor exploited the situation created by the war of the European powers, just as his forbear had benefited from Anglo-French hostilities in Elizabethan times. He declared himself to be 'at war' with all countries not consularly represented in his domains – and dunned all and sundry for tribute. In 1800, his ships captured a Prussian vessel in local waters, held master and crew to ransom, and thus forced Prussia to post a consul to Tangier. Even supposedly friendly powers were dunned as well: when an American vessel, the *Oswego*, ran aground off Mogador that year, Captain Paddock and his seven men were tossed in jail. Simpson reported that the ransom he negotiated – forty dollars for Paddock, twenty for each of the men – was unusually low and proved his excellent relations with the Court: but it probably reflected, more, the Court's estimate of how much could be coaxed from Philadelphia for a non-scheduled item in the limited foreign affairs budget.

Nevertheless, when the local Catholic diocese treasurer asked two thousand dollars for a lot on which Simpson wanted to build a permanent consulate, his relations with the Emperor were good enough for the royal family to offer him any of three choicer lots for six hundred dollars. Unfortunately, when Simpson chose the most attractive, overlooking Tangier landing, he found that the princeling owner had already sold the same site to the British consul, who protested. Simpson and the princeling won the ensuing dispute.

Actual consular correspondence, then, out of Barbary, was not extensive – perhaps six or seven reports per year from every post – but they were crowded with housekeeping details. The U.S. representatives lived a hand-to-mouth existence and wrote constantly about money and housing. They ordered their exotic stores – tea, cinnamon water, liquor – from war-torn

Europe as best they could The highlight of the year was when the American squadron – two or three warships – sailed through the Straits. These vessels usually found it safer to water at Tangier or Tetuan than at European ports which, except for Gibraltar – which had no natural water supply – were often blockaded by Nelson's fleet.

For Morocco, the war situation was a mixed blessing: the country's slaving and other illicit traffic had to be disguised, to obtain 'passports' (safe-conducts) from the naval powers. In 1802, Sweden and the United States purposely delayed on requests from Sultan Soliman for naval passports to enter 'Tripoly', which was then blockaded. The choleric Emperor decided to go to war with both countries. No shots were fired; but on June 25, Commander Richard Morris, U.S.N., reported Simpson's arrival at The Rock: his fellow-consul had been ejected from the kingdom and carried Soliman's declaration of hostilities. Morris nervously asked Minister Rufus King in London for a third warship.

By year's end, the King had called an end to his war with the United States and Simpson had resumed residence in Tangier; but relations remained cool thereafter. Philadelphia mollified Soliman by honoring an earlier promise – a gift of one hundred gun carriages. Soliman took advantage of Simpson's appearance at Court to berate him for his failure to make a biennial horseback visit, bearing gifts. The United States learned early that Africa's affection for the outside world can often be a highly intrinsic, marketable commodity.

One of Jefferson's first acts, on becoming President in 1801, was to cut Army expenditure and reduce the Navy to six ships. On the Barbary Shore, this exposed American merchant crews to even more pillage and enslavement than before. Piracy – at this period, the main revenue-producing industry of the Maghreb – added to a problem created by U.S. independence itself: the loss of British naval protection.

The 1795 treaty with Algiers included the payment of substantial ransom for American captives; the *Dey* had taken over a dozen United States merchantmen in the past ten years, and held over a hundred American slaves at the time of the accord. The Tripoli treaty of 1796 was broadly similar in terms, and the 1797 pact with Tunis was even more expensive in ransom money. The slogan 'millions for defense but not one cent for

9

tribute' was being effectively flouted – and the treaties themselves were to prove of little effective value.

The Tripolitan War between the *Bey*'s dominions and the United States lasted from 1801 to 1805. It began when the *Bey* had the U.S. Consulate-General flagpole chopped down and Consul-General James Leander Cathcart expelled. Today, the Marines remember Tripoli with the same pride as Montezuma, but Tripoli barely remembers them: America prosecuted the war listlessly; Secretary of State Madison's hope was to restore Hamet Caramalli against his usurping brother, Joseph; but the war ended, without the achievement of this goal, on a nominal victory. The United States simply announced that it had won, setting a precedent in the search for peace that was to come in handy 167 years later, in southeast Asia.

A new treaty was made in 1805, but sixty thousand dollars ransom money had to be paid again for prisoners. Piracy and kidnapping continued. After the U.S. Mediterranean squadron was withdrawn in 1807, American shipping, for the next eight years, was to find itself, in Condé's words, 'virtually defenseless'.

In March, 1815, Congress authorized war against Algiers, which had already begun hostilities with the Republic three years before. Commodore Decatur effectively won the shooting aspects of this war, thus encouraging the European states to take on the corsair problem more seriously: but Joel Barlow, agent to David Humphreys in Portugal, had to negotiate heavy ransom once again. The President was authorized to borrow sums of one million dollars and $325,000, and also received an appropriation of $260,000 – all of this to buy off the *Dey*, Omar Pasha.

The new treaty, drafted in English, was signed at the end of the year by the ruler and by U.S. Consul William Shaler. An almost identical agreement, this time with the original in Turkish script, was signed by Shaler, Navy Commander Isaac Chauncey and the *Dey* the following year.

Down the Afric Shore

Meanwhile, Yankee ships took advantage of the Napoleonic wars to develop legitimate trade and slaving – still, itself, technically legitimate in most of the American states – on the coast of Atlantic Africa, the so-called 'Afric shore', especially Senegal and Sierra Leone. The first main American items of trade were rum and tobacco, followed in importance by guns and gunpowder and (in Muslim markets like Senegal) white cloth – elsewhere, the more garish European waxprint cottons were more popular. The main trading ports for west Africa in the United States were then Salem, Massachusetts, and Newport, Rhode Island.

The Anglo-American convention on commerce and navigation of 1815 later forbade American ships from trading with the British possessions in Africa, meaning the trading forts on the Atlantic coast and the small settlement at the Cape. Yankee schooners continued to revictual in these places, however. Incipient protectionism by the proto-colonial powers could often be evaded with the connivance of European traders, and this in turn forced compromise. On June 18, 1812, the Congress declared war on Britain – to the dismay of Yankee traders on the African Atlantic coast. But some Anglo-American commerce continued unabated for a while, and was quickly re-established when the fighting ended.

In 1822, Gorée, off Senegal, became an island *entrepôt* for American goods, with the official approval of France, the main foreign power. British pre-colonial protectionism was rather more rigid, the British navy being better able to enforce such trade monopolies.

These were the salad days of the Yankee traders. For them, the Atlantic was a no-man's-land which offered roughly equal opportunity to major power and ex-colony alike. Of the various Atlantic markets, Africa was the one that offered the most unfettered form of cut-throat competition.

In the nineteenth century, Africa never took more than one per cent of American exports; but America's trading *share* of Atlantic Africa was often high. For the first three-quarters of the century, American goods totaled over half of all imports into Senegal. Smuggling included, they were a substantial part of Gambian trade. By the 1860's, U.S. exports accounted for nearly half the imports into the Gold Coast, despite frequent friction with the British forts. In Liberia, U.S. ships had a clear advantage. Africa's main exports were gold dust, palm oil and kernels, ivory, hides and peanuts.

The Gold Coast was the most valuable market, followed by Liberia, then by the *entrepôts* at Gorée, Bathurst and Freetown, and those on the Nuñez and Pongo estuaries. Sale was on credit, with goods put ashore on the down journey, and barter collected coming up the Coast. After the Berlin Conference, U.S. trade declined against European competition, as it had done during the Civil War, to revive again during the first world conflict. The historian George Brooks notes interestingly that tobacco and liquor attracted more buyers than the products of 'technology' – a factor favoring rural America over urban Europe.

Rhode Island and Massachusetts abolished slaving in 1788. Although this did not entirely prevent merchants in either state from trading in slaves, it did encourage the drift toward legitimate commerce. The French Revolution outlawed slavery in 1794, but Napoleon re-established it in 1802, directing it toward Hispaniola, Guadeloupe and Martinique. In west Africa, French rule was resented in Saint-Louis and particularly on Gorée island where there were popular attempts to prevent France's return after Waterloo. Gorée was finally returned to France in 1817. At the time, American schooners concentrated on the Gorée–St. Louis–Gambia River–Freetown–Los Islands circuit.

Traders, American and European, were a nationality apart: although frequently at loggerheads, they were more or less united in their enmity for authority. Indeed, at the time, the notion of major governments, far away, attempting to apply their authority down the African coast must have seemed quaintly absurd to seafaring people on the spot, hazarding their lives for trade. Governor Sir Charles MacCarthy, ruling all the British settlements from Freetown, reported to Lord Bathurst at the Foreign Office on July 12, 1815, that St. James Fort on the Gambia River would have to be militarily reoccupied, otherwise 'the whole of the important trade of that river will soon be in the hands of the Americans'. British troops were sent to the little fortress island the following year. Mac-Carthy was emotionally anti-Republican and anti-American, and he viewed with dismay the huge growth of American trade with the Windward Coast – the area in the trade winds belt – after the war of 1812.

Most Windward Coast trading was confined to the period from November to May, when breeze and weather were favorable and the absence of rains brought indigenous traders down from the interior – although the season was also marked by the *harmattan*, the sand-bearing wind which was a hazard to navigation, and by high seas close in.

Many of the American ships on the Coast were of sixty tons or less (measured then by keel to waterline length, rather than by real displacement) with a crew of half a dozen or fewer. A brig might have a captain, two officers, five or six seamen, a Negro or African cook and a cabin boy. Larger ships employed a supercargo, but this task usually fell to the captain or first mate.

In 1818, a U.S. career consul was appointed to Porto Praia on São Jago in the Cabo Verdes. Four years later, Samuel Hodges Jr., of Stoughton, Massachusetts, set up a prosperous commission business on the island: he traded both with 'legitimates' and with smugglers all along the Coast, from Mauritania to Sierra Leone. In 1843, Matthew Perry became commodore of the first U.S. African squadron, with a mandate to check slaving – but with authority to stop and search only American ships.

The campaign against slaving across the world had received its primary impetus from a decision, in 1772, by Lord Mansfield, Britain's Chief Justice, that slaving was illicit in the United Kingdom. In 1794, the Congress forbade the outfitting of slaving ships in America if they were destined to carry slaves from one foreign country to another. In 1800, American citizens themselves were denied the right to carry slaves from one foreign country to another – in any ship. In 1807, slaving to the United States was interdicted. The same year, British ships were forbidden to slave.

The events that brought the U.S. African squadron into being began on June 12, 1839, when Lieutenant Charles Fitzgerald of the British navy brought his brig *Buzzard* into New York with two captured American slavers *Beagle* and *Clara*. A

United States marshal arrested the crews but the Britons were told to keep the ships as prizes. Two weeks later, the British brig *Harlequin* brought in the slaver *Wyoming*, whose captain had had a heart attack and died on arrest. In the fall, the brig *Dolphin* brought in *Butterfly* and *Catherine*.

The British commanders had clearly decided to force a showdown over the use of the Stars and Stripes by filling New York harbor with captured slave shipping. In all the cases, crews and owners were clearly Spanish: the American captains and U.S. flags were obviously a convenience, nothing more – to try to inhibit the Royal Navy from boarding and searching. But the Vice-Admiralty Court of Mixed Commission in Freetown had refused to judge the vessels, ruling that although Spain had agreed to British jurisdiction, the U.S. had not. Hence, the British commanders claimed, judgment should be given against the crews and vessels in New York. President Van Buren gave instructions that the New York district attorney, Benjamin F. Butler, should 'prosecute, if he can'.

Butler decided that, since *Beagle* and *Clara* were obviously clearly Spanish, he could not seize them. Fitzgerald took them to the vice-admiralty court in Bermuda, which also refused the case, then to Freetown again, losing the *Beagle* in a storm but finally securing court seizure of the *Clara*.

The *Clara* decision ended the false use of United States ships papers for a while. Meanwhile, back in New York, Butler had changed his mind and had successfully prosecuted *Wyoming*, *Butterfly* and *Catherine*, seizing the ships; the prisoners, however, slipped bail.

That year, Robert W. Allen and John Henderson of Baltimore were arrested as co-owners of the *Catherine*. Along with a Francis T. Montell, owner of the slaver *Elvira*, they were tried – as was, the following year, John F. Strohm, builder of the slaving schooner *Ann*. Pro-slaving juries pronounced acquittals in both cases, to the fury of Maryland's Chief Justice, Roger B. Taney: but Allen lost his ship's registry bond.

Van Buren, State Secretary John Forsyth and their successors, President John Tyler and Secretary Daniel Webster later reversed the unfavorable attitude toward British search and seizure, but agreed to set up a U.S. squadron to help police U.S. shipping. Under the Webster–Ashburton treaty of 1842, ships from the British and American squadrons were to cruise together: but this arrangement rarely worked, as the heavier American ships, built for coastal defense, could rarely surpass six knots and were left behind when a chase began. The bounty for recapturing slaves was twentyfive dollars a head – less than the British navy's competing rate. Navy Secretary Abel B. Upshur – who, like most of his nineteenth century successors, was a southerner – warned Perry against overzealousness in checking slaving by telling him not to inflict 'injurious and vexatious interruptions' on legal traders. Owners of ships held, then released, sometimes brought damage suits against individual officers – even if the ships were genuine slavers which had dodged seizure on a legal technicality. For this and other intimidating reasons, the squadron was not particularly successful in checking slaving. The Betts court in New York was notorious for selling acquittals to wealthy slavers. But in 1848, Captain Nathaniel Gordon of the *Erie* became the only American slaving skipper ever to die for his offense when he was hanged in Baltimore under an Act of Congress passed as far back as 1820.

The American squadron saw little fire. In 1844, it showed the flag for a month at Bissau to protect American goods during a revolt, before being forced to withdraw by fever. Earlier, it intervened energetically in the Ivory Coast to protect American traders, and in Liberia to defend the vulnerable Maryland Colonization Society settlement at Cape Palmas.

Americans nationalistically objected to foreign men-of-war searching United States vessels, especially if the alien warships were British: in 1858, Britain renounced the right to search U.S. ships – a decision which persuaded nearly all slaving ships to hoist the Stars and Stripes again, whenever a British ship gave chase. The anti-slaving operation was back to square one: but not for long.

Both the growth of trade and reluctant awareness of the need to repress slaving made a permanent American official presence on the Coast desirable. Consular agents, usually traders or traders' representatives, were appointed by the consuls at Praia. The first was at Bathurst in 1834, where peanuts had come to dominate trade and where the United States bought well over half the crop. In the best years, American ships would drop sail at Bathurst approximately once a week. W. M. Haxton, appointed on October 17, 1833, took up office the following February. He was largely inactive, presumably because of ill health, and was succeeded by Daniel R. B. Upton. The post was later downgraded to a commercial agency, then raised to a Vice-Consulate before being closed in 1900, when it was merged with the Consulate at Gorée.

In 1858, a consular officer was named at Freetown – John E. Taylor, who had been informally appointed by Commodore Mayo of the U.S. African squadron five years before. In 1857, a French trader, Adolphe Demay, was appointed consular agent in Bissau by Consul W. H. Morse: this encouraged a trader, John B. Upton, to set up shop there the following year. He later moved to Freetown.

Squadron commodores, like the U.S. naval liaison officer at Gibraltar today, had quasi-consular status: Mayo, who commanded 1853–54, himself appointed acting United States Consuls at Freetown, Bathurst and Luanda. He also negotiated a treaty with King Docemo of Lagos, giving America most-favored-nation treatment in the King's domains.

Consular agents received no compensation except the right to levy dues for specific tasks, such as witnessing documents. But their appointments gave them status in dealing with European officials; and, as Brooks suggests, the posts also undoubtedly provided their incumbents with the means to inform themselves of the activities of other American businessmen. One of the most consistently manned consular agencies was Freetown: representatives of U.S. companies who served in this capacity there in the Fifties and Sixties included the Englishman, James P. Kidd, and the Americans, John B. Upton, George K. Benedict and Henry Rider, who was succeeded by Henry Randall. From 1879 to 1889, the post was held by Judson A. Lewis. The laying of the Atlantic cable in 1866 considerably facilitated consular reporting from Praia.

By mid-century, the main staples of the American trade to Atlantic Africa remained tobacco and rum. The Gambia's highly favorable trade balance with the U.S. declined in 1842, when the Congress imposed a tax of thirtytwo cents a bushel on foreign peanuts: the f.o.b. price at the time averaged fiftyfive cents a bushel. As a port, Bathurst had never been very popular with American crews because of its poor health record.

In 1952, however, France made Gorée a free port for all imports except cloth. American-made imports rose from *Frs.* 30,940 to *Frs.* 345,877 in 1855. They then remained consistently around this level. A Captain Henry Skinner established a commission agency on the island, and also processed cotton there. Peanuts from the Senegalese mainland were the main export.

Also in 1852, American specie were made legal tender in the British settlements, with the dollar valued at just over four shillings – an exchange rate that continued for nearly a century, until the second world war. The recovery in U.S.–African trade after the Civil War was particularly noticeable on Gorée island, where imports from the U.S. once again surpassed in value those of France and other countries. Although trade with the French settlement declined with the Franco-Prussian war, traders' representative Peter Strickland of Boston lived and traded on Gorée in the Seventies and Eighties, and became in 1883 the first honorary U.S. Consul on the island.

Down-latitude, on the Leeward Coast, American and European traders were largely restricted to their ships. Most trading negotiations were conducted through Kru from Liberia or other 'talk-men': native 'gold-takers' were employed to test gold dust. Most coastal trading settlements were native-run. Trade with the Leeward Coast, where American interests dated from the late eighteenth century corsair Dudley Saltonstall, was more risky and difficult than up the Coast, but could often be more profitable. In Governor MacCarthy's day, relations with the British were usually difficult, especially when the Danish government briefly toyed with the notion of disposing of their forts – including Christiansborg at Accra – to the American Colonization Society, founders of Liberia. The main American import from the Leeward Coast was palm oil (expressed locally from palm husks) and palm kernels, from which a higher quality oil was extracted mechanically in the United States.

Most U.S. trade was in sailing ships, which were handicapped in competition with the new British steamers. When this competition was overcome, growing protectionist tariffs imposed by the proto-colonial powers provided a fresh hurdle, and U.S. Consuls had little leverage. The best they could do was to turn as much of a blind eye as possible to the natural result of high tariffs – smuggling.

A more original reaction to protectionism came in 1879 when Joseph Upton and William Stephens of the bark *James A. Herriman* negotiated a ninetynine-year lease on part of Denu (now in modern Ghana) for five hundred dollars a year. They sent their 'treaty' with the Denu chief to Washington for approval. The British successfully protested that Denu was within their internationally agreed sphere of influence.

There was relatively little American trade in the Biafran Bight, essentially the province of European, and predominantly British, 'palm oil ruffians', or farther south – a long haul for the Porto Praia squadron, with a slow return against unfavorable winds. However, Peter F. Evers, Richard J. Arnold, Daniel Greene and Elijah J. Pierce, all of Rhode Island, made an attempted exploratory ascent of the Niger, starting at the Nun Channel, in 1833. The bid was defeated by the inadequacy of sail power, by the loyalty of King Boy, the Delta chief, to his agreement with the Lander brothers (the British youths who had made the original Niger charting expedition in 1827) and by fever.

Spreading farther, American ships traded with Principe and São Tomé, but found the Portuguese traders – Europeans and Eurafricans – exceptionally dishonest in comparison to the African traders on the mainland. An American presence in the form of an Episcopalian mission was established among the tidewater mangroves on the north bank of the Gabun estuary in 1842, and soon came under French pressures.

By the end of the nineteenth century, American trade was largely restricted to Senegal, Sierra Leone and the Gold Coast. The age of small traders had by then nearly disappeared: the cancerous growth of imperial protectionism was choking free trade – but without, in some cases, quite killing American commerce. Brooks quotes Gold Coast documents to show the great importance of the duty on American rum in running that colony's budget in the 1890's. A U.S. consular agency existed at Elmina from 1879 to 1900. After that, it was not until 1928 that a mission was re-established on the Leeward Coast – a consulate in Lagos. Farther south, an acting consulate existed in the Gabun from 1856 to 1888, and in Boma, the Congo Estuary port, from 1888 onward, until the move to Leopoldville.

Yankees under Capricorn

Across the continent, in Capricorn Africa, Americans were scarcely less active than they were in Atlantic Africa. The competition was also similar. The restrictions on U.S. trade with the Cape imposed by the 1815 treaty with the British led to the 1833 agreement between the United States and Seyyid Said, Sultan of Muscat, Oman and Zanzibar.

The negotiator of this historic document was Consul Edmund Roberts, a special agent with a roving Indian Ocean commission. His agreement fixed duty on American goods at five per cent, gave protection to U.S. citizens and property, and provided for a consulate to be established. (It was set up in 1836 or early 1837, and lasted until 1906.)

The Zanzibar treaty, which was to lead to American ships out-trading those of any European nation in the area for three decades, was signed at Muscat, as the accord preceded the division of the sultanate between Said's two sons and heirs. Roberts, a trader, had been to Zanzibar in 1827 with the *Mary Ann*, chartered from New Bedford, and had suffered commercially from Britain's quasi-monopoly of island trade. When the Sultan visited from Muscat in January 1828, Roberts obtained an audience. The Sultan welcomed the notion of foreign powers competing for his favors and sought American arms with which to fight his main colonial competitors, the Portuguese. The Muscati ruler himself proposed the commercial treaty.

When the New Hampshire senator, Levi Woodbury, a personal friend of Roberts', became Secretary of the Navy in March 1831, the road toward obtaining President Jackson's consent to the drafting of a treaty was open. Because of uncertainty over the remote ruler's health and perhaps over spelling, blanks were left in the document for the Sultan's name to be inserted. Roberts sailed to Muscat aboard a ship of war, the *Peacock*, creating a spate of rumors of 'Yankee expansionism' among the British at the Cape – where his 'cover', as clerk to the captain, at fifteen hundred dollars a year, appears to have been easily 'blown'. This was in 1833, and Roberts was to return to Zanzibar in 1835 with the Senate's ratification. The Salem merchants moved swiftly to insure that the

Zanzibar Consul should be chosen from their community: their townsman, Richard P. Waters, was appointed. Waters, himself a businessman, formed an alliance with the master of the Sultan's customs house, Jairam Sewejee (from his name, presumably an Indian), whereby both men received a commission on the now virtually duty-free American imports. The rival British trading firm of Newman, Hunt and Christopher soon closed down, and the Salem merchants, particularly the partners John Bertram and Michael Shepard – known in Zanzibar as 'the Big Firm' – prospered. In 1841, Britain appointed a permanent consul who obtained equal rights for British traders the following year: but not until the Civil War, which kept American ships at home and directed export industries toward the domestic needs of the rival armies, did British trade again surpass that of the United States.

On April 3, 1841, a bark belonging to the Sultan and called the *as-Sultanah*, flying the scarlet Zanzibari ensign, docked at New York, taking advantage of the 'reciprocal' terms of the Roberts treaty. The voyage, possibly the first by an African ship across the Atlantic, was encouraged by New York merchants seeking to challenge the trading power of Massachusetts. The bark's master, Ahmad bin Na'aman, was lionized by mercantile society, and the U.S. Navy dockyard helped repair the ship for its return. Ahmad was later referred to in British consular reports as the 'leader of the American party' in Zanzibar. Salem and New York traders prospered, and appointed agents in Madagascar, Mozambique and Aden. Later, however, competition from Rufus Greene of Providence and from the Hamburg 'cauri' firm of William O'Swald was to reduce profit margins for the Salem and New York merchants.

U.S.–Zanzibari relations grew fractious during the consulship of Charles Ward in the late 'forties: on the Fourth of July 1850, when the Sultan canceled a public salute to the Stars and Stripes, Ward brusquely closed the Consulate. The following year, the U.S.S. *Susquehanna*, commanded by John Aulick, anchored off Zanzibar Town and threatened to bombard it unless an apology was received. The Sultan acquiesced. A new and more diplomatic consul, John F. Webb, was then appointed to restore friendly relations. By 1859, thirtyfive of eighty foreign ships calling at Zanzibar that year were American, aggregating trade of over two hundred thousand dollars. By then, however, U.S. commerce with the Cape had resumed as well, and was worth – according to a recent estimate by Laurence Howard – seven hundred and fifty thousand dollars annually.

Nineteenth century American trade with other parts of the Indian Ocean also was significant. Links with Mauritius had predated British rule, from the time when it was the Ile de France. The French-educated Polish adventurer Count Beny-owski, who ruled a kingdom in northern Madagascar shortly after U.S. independence, came to Paris for financial support in the 1870's and collected letters of recommendation from Ambassador Benjamin Franklin. He arrived in Baltimore in the *Robert and Ann*, and later returned to his fief with American followers.

Eventually, French troops invaded the kingdom, killing Benyowski in combat on May 7, 1786. His American followers were shot that day or hunted down in the weeks that followed. Even earlier, the six-nation 'pirate republic' of Libertalia in northern Madagascar had had trading links with the Carolinas.

By mid-century, U.S. trade was still dominant in East Africa and probably in Liberia; it was second to that of the United Kingdom in the Cape and to Portugal in Portuguese Africa. It was still significant elsewhere. Howard puts annual American trade in west Africa, including smuggling, at around the four million-dollar mark in this period, but this looks like an under-estimate: Niger Delta oil alone was worth twelve million dollars a year by 1845, and a substantial portion of this was going to American soap factories.

Liberia: Birth of a Nation

South Africa and especially Liberia were cases apart. A consulate with almost exclusively maritime concerns existed from 1799 in Cape Town – then the only U.S. mission south of the

Equator. The first American trading schooner anchored at the Cape in 1784: for fifty years, the waters of the area were a center for New England whalers. In the five years preceding the Cape Town consulate, 124 American ships tied up in the harbor.

Liberia was naturally a much greater center of American interests and activity. Its conception was intended to solve the problem of the poverty of freed slaves in the United States. It was also meant to remove the political problem they posed as a challenge to the property and safety of slave-owning whites. Thus, philanthropists and some slave owners both saw 'African zionism' as an answer to their problems. Liberia was the historical creation of the slave trade: its growth was to be checked by slavery's demise in the United States. Had slavery died a generation sooner than Appomattox, Liberia's birth would probably never have taken place.

The first initiative toward emigration to Africa had been undertaken in 1815 by a Quaker Negro ship's master, Paul Cuffee of Westport, Massachusetts. Cuffee's name – presumably originally Kofi, a West African name meaning a boy born on Friday – reflects the fact that he was only second generation American. Cuffee did not envisage an African 'homeland' for black Americans, but merely sought to establish a Negro trading *élite* on the Leeward Coast, to develop trans-Atlantic commerce.

He had made his first two voyages to the Freetown, Sierra Leone, settlement in 1811 – receiving encouragement, in between, from liberals he had met in London. On the second trip, he had initial difficulties winning a relaxation, in Sierra Leone, of the virtual British embargo on American trade. The approach of war had made animosities acute.

Early in 1812, he had sailed for home: four days out of Freetown, he was seized by a British naval patrol, whose commander asserted that three African apprentices among Cuffee's crew were really slaves. Returned to Freetown, his ship was released on orders from Governor Zachary Macaulay. Back at Westport, the U.S. customs seized the ship again because of the newly passed 'Non-Intercourse Act', forbidding trade with British ports; but Cuffee took a seat in the Washington coach from Newport and obtained a personal audience with President Madison and Treasury Secretary Albert Gallatin. His ship was again released.

His third trip with nine families – thirtyeight colonists – was frustrated for several months by the war of 1812. The resourceful Cuffee had a special bill drafted, in 1814, permitting him to go to the British port of Freetown in spite of the war; this bill passed the Senate, but the House rejected the proposal by seven votes, and he had to wait for the war to end.

At a personal loss of four thousand dollars, he sailed his ship, the *Traveler*, for Sierra Leone, on December 10, 1815. The venture was only a marginal success. The remarkable pioneer made a fourth trip to Freetown, with emigrants, in 1816, and died in Westport the following year.

Following difficult tractations, a purely American settlement was finally established at Cape Mesurado, the heart of contemporary Liberia, in the 1820's. There was opposition from Governor MacCarthy to an American settlement being created near Freetown, and it was this that led to the choice of Mesurado – although the spot was even more unsuitable, initially, than Freetown had been. Ample histories of the Mesurado settlement's difficulties exist. In retrospect, viewing the problems of health and native hostility that plagued the Liberian pioneers, it is hard to understand why Spain's bid to sell Fernando Póo, in 1831, for one hundred thousand pounds – about half a million dollars – was never taken up, once Britain had turned down the offer. The island's security and salubrity, plus its well-established role in trade and chandlering, would have seemed to make it an ideal choice for a colonization settlement.

Liberia's early history continued to be fragile and its relationship with the U.S. uncertain. In 1828, the newly elected President Andrew Jackson made Amos Kendall of Kentucky a Treasury auditor, responsible for naval expenditures. In 1830, Kendall presented a report on the American Agency in Liberia. Concluding that the Agency had exceeded its mandate, Kendall said the transport of 'less than 260' Negroes had already cost $264,710 – more than a thousand dollars a head. Funds were consequently cut by Congress. In 1832, the decision was taken to liquidate the Agency.

U.S. responsibility for Liberia was always clearly reluctant, especially when it ran counter to relations with longer-established states. Independence, in 1847, was virtually forced on

Liberia by Washington. Much of the American attitude stemmed from a laudable reluctance to colonize. The Declaration of Independence had said that 'governments derive their just powers from the consent of the governed' and that when any form of government destroyed the 'natural rights of man' it was the 'right of the people to alter or abolish it': there was therefore an inbuilt dislike of anything that might resemble imperial rule. (Lawrence Howard argues that the U.S. did in fact have imperial aims in Liberia: but his arguments presume that the use of force to capture land – the normal political activity of even the smallest chiefdoms in Africa – is 'imperialistic'. Not all conquest is colonialism.)

On the official side, the U.S. appointed a commercial agent, James W. Lugenbeel, at Monrovia in 1848. The post became a Legation and Consulate-General in 1862, by which time there were no less than twentyfive U.S. Consuls and agents in Africa. A 'Commissioner and Consul-General', John J. Henry, arrived the following year, with consular agencies being established at Grand Bassa in 1868, and later at Cape Palmas. In 1879, a part-time consular agency at Elmina on the Gold Coast, headed by Trader P. S. Hamel and later by Trader Arthur Brunn (who also represented France and the Netherlands) was placed under the jurisdiction of Monrovia – whose Minister was the ranking American foreign service officer in the dark continent, and the ranking black American in the Washington administration. The Elmina post became full-time in 1883 under a Gold Coaster, George E. Eminsang; it was finally closed in 1900.

Missionaries and Adventurers

The dynamism of Yankee traders in Africa often provoked European fears of America's real intentions. Liberia at first encouraged, then proved the baselessness of these fears. Two Americans, however, did try to impose an administration on the mid-Atlantic island of Tristan da Cunha in the 1840's.

They were Jonathan Lambert and Richard Cleveland, both of Salem. It was hardly an imperial aim in the normal sense, since the scheme had the support of the six families which made up the island's population – Nelsonian marines, Eurafrican women from the Cape, and their children. (The descendants of these pioneers are the 200-plus Tristanians of today.) Lambert and Cleveland were unsuccessful: Britain, which had neglected the island, now asserted its dominion.

Religion also enjoyed a considerable role in nineteenth century U.S. links with Africa. Just as the Quaker Cuffee had played a part in Sierra Leone, other devout protestants loomed large in the founding of Liberia – finally established through a pistol-point agreement with local chiefs, in 1824, by Lieutenant Robert Stockton of the U.S.S. *Alligator*. (After many frustrating weeks of tribal chicanery, Stockton finally held his weapon to the head of someone described as 'King Peter' in the records. The King signed land over to Dr Eli Ayres, the American Colonization Society's white resident agent.)

Initially, progress came so slowly that the early settlement could be justly called a failure. Clendenen and Duignan have described how Negro missionaries were sent to Africa in the wake of the colony's foundation, on the assumption that they would be better accepted and would have a stronger resistance to tropical disease. They conclude: 'None of these assumptions was true. Immunity to disease proved to be an individual matter, rather than a racial characteristic, and the death toll among the Negro American missionaries was as frightful as among the white men. To the native African, the Negro American was not a compatriot but another foreigner – and a foreigner who had much more in common with the white men that he did with any African. Cultural ties between the American and African Negroes were practically non-existent.'

In 1843, the American Board of Missions transfered from Cape Palmas, Liberia, to the Gabun; but a minor international conflict developed almost at once: the following year, a French naval officer procured the signature of a native chief in the same village on a 'treaty' with France. As the chief was illiterate – and, according to mission testimony, drunk at the time – the natives later refused to let the French ashore when they returned to set up an 'administration'. A gunboat hurled shells into the fragile huts, apparently purposely damaging the mission church, and ignoring the U.S. flag. The mission's boats were reportedly stolen by French officers. But threats of 'expulsion' by the French came to nothing. Commodore George C. Read, then commanding the U.S. African squadron, arrived in the little equatorial beauty-spot in 1846 and dealt sternly with the French officers. A French admiral later came to the mission to apologize. What the missionaries had feared the most – competition from a 'romanist' mission – never transpired.

The evangelization of western Nigeria owes a great deal to the American Baptist, Thomas Jefferson Bowen, a former Republic of Texas cavalry captain who was ordained in the early 1840's and went to Yorubaland in 1849: he survived through humor, toughness and occasionally pistol skill. The area was wracked at the time by Egba Yoruba warfare, in which he helped his newfound friends with his military talents. He returned to the United States in 1852, married, and went back with his bride to Ogbomosho the following year, finally retiring to America because of ill health in 1856. By then his skills as explorer and linguist had enabled him to transliterate Yoruba, one of black Africa's three or four most spoken indigenous tongues.

Protestant medical missionaries first sailed for South Africa in 1834, encouraged by the Zulu kings Dingaan and Mosalekatsi. The main mission moved out to Moseka and soon found itself in the path of a *boer* raid on Mosalekatsi's lands. Although Mosalekatsi initially repulsed the *boers* (Dutch-origin European settlers), their bloody emergence in the region made suspicion fall on all whites, and the mission had to return to the coast – Dingaan's country.

But *boer* predations persisted, forcing Dingaan, also, to abandon his initial friendly policy toward white strangers. When Dingaan's spearmen killed the Piet Retief raiding party, and the king prepared to defend himself from the gathering horde, he offered the American and other missionaries his royal protection: but the missionaries feared that this benevolence might not last in the face of the *boer* invasion.

After some soul-searching, the American party returned to the United States, leaving behind Daniel Lindley to try to evangelize the *boers*. Later, American missions were re-established in South Africa: here, even more than elsewhere,

26

missionaries were a major force for transliterating the languages of the country and studying local culture.

Adventure was a spur almost as strong as faith in bringing nineteenth century Americans to Africa. American explorers included John Ledyard and Archibald Robbins of Connecticut: the latter, enslaved in Mauritania after shipwreck, traveled three years with nomads and later wrote of his experiences. Americans also sometimes served in the colonial forces of European countries, even including Portugal's.

Perhaps the best-known American explorer before Stanley was Paul Belloni du Chaillu, a French-born Philadelphian who spent his childhood with his French trader-father in the Gabun. He emigrated to the U.S. in the early 1850's, became a citizen, and returned to Mpongwe country in 1855 as a self-styled 'scientific explorer'. He has his niche in history as the man who discovered the gorilla. Like most of the early African explorers, his discoveries – including gorillas – were doubted by the armchair savants, and even by the great Anglo-German explorer of west Africa, Heinrich Barth (who knew, of course, nothing about equatorial Africa.) On a second journey in 1863, Belloni du Chaillu managed to bring back a (dead) gorilla and also rediscovered pygmies – whose existence was first recorded by the Phoenicians. Uninformed criticism of him began to wane.

America never established so much as an acre of African colony or even of officially protected trading post; but, as Clendenan and Duignan have pointed out, 'the impact of the United States upon Africa as a whole was probably as decisive in its ultimate effects as that of any other (foreign) country'. What nineteenth century writers sometimes called the 'Ethiope factor' in American foreign intercourse had proved to be a constant, even fairly important element in policy. Africa, like America, was a continent of frontiersmen, black and white, and one of the few areas of the global scene where the domination of Europe was not assured. The role of American traders and missionaries in Africa was as great as those of any European state's merchants and men of God: misguided fears of American imperial ambitions helped fire the genuine empire-building dynamism of France, Britain, Belgium, Italy, Portugal and Spain.

The Eve of Colonial Rule

In North Africa, the U.S. consuls were more concerned with affairs related to global strategy and to Europe. On August 26, 1865, we find Charles Hale, Consul-General in Alexandria, informing Secretary of State Seward – still convalescing from the wound sustained a few months before, during Lincoln's assassination – with news, obtained from missionaries in Nubia, that the French were recruiting Sudanese from the Pasha of Egypt's dominions to help their attempt to establish rule over Mexico. Hale had urged that the number of black soldiers sent should be kept as few as was consonant with the Pasha's financial needs from Paris.

From Washington, Seward instructed Hale to lean on the Pasha harder – to tell him that, with Abolition, the U.S. could no longer tolerate 'civil or military servitude in this hemisphere'. The aid of Colonel Stanton, the British Consul-General, was recruited to help press the point. At the time, any Egyptian slave who could reach the British post and kiss the flag was sent to the local court with a *dragoman* (major-domo) to demand emancipation papers under the Pasha's abolition agreement – forced on him earlier by Britain.

In November, some of the Nubian conscripts revolted in the south, and Hale reported on the 13th that the plan to send nine hundred to Mexico had been abandoned. On the 16th, the Pasha seems to have back-pedaled once again, saying that the reinforcements would have to go, but stressing that this was the last contingent of its sort. It was to replace Nubians already in service in the French army in Mexico who were due home: the nine hundred, he affirmed, were not slaves, but conscripts. After an exchange of hair-splitting letters between all parties about the exact civil status of the riflemen, Hale was able to report on November 27 that the French frigate *Ardèche* had sailed for Marseille without them.

In Tunis at this time, Consul Amos Perry discovered the *Bey* to be markedly more genuine in his opposition to slavery than the Pasha. In Tangier, still a cardinal post, we find Consul-General Jesse H. McMath busy requesting funds to pay America's annual share ($285) toward the upkeep of the new Cape Spartel lighthouse – with Dakar, Cape Town and

Cape Guardafui, one of the main four lighthouses in Africa – and hoping that the cholera epidemic would not spread to Tangier from Gibraltar. The war between the States had little resonance in this area, except the decision for Abolition, which was to affect official American attitudes toward traditional slave-holding societies around the world.

After the Civil War watershed in United States relations with black Africa, American trade severely declined, both in the Capricorn area and on 'the Coast'. Emancipation almost entirely removed Negro–American interest in emigration to the old continent. A Liberian revolt in 1871 (put down by the Americo-Liberians with assistance from a U.S. warship) made this old new frontier even less attractive.

Calls for American military assistance by Monrovia became more frequent. The U.S. helped to defend the Liberian government against the threat of French encroachment in the late Seventies. In 1879, the U.S. again navally intervened to put down a Grebo rising aimed at bringing in British administration. In 1882, a flotilla of British gunboats under Sir Arthur Havelock, Governor of Sierra Leone, threatened to bombard Monrovia over a border claim and damage to British traders' property by tribes over whom the Liberian government had no control: President Chester A. Arthur intervened for Liberia, but was clearly unprepared to match force with force. Finally, British troops occupied the contested zone.

U.S. Minister John H. Smyth unsuccessfully intervened against a French official land seizure in Liberia in 1886 – based on a French 'treaty' of that year with local chiefs in which the last two figures of the date were impressively reversed, to suggest a more longstanding French association. In this case, the contested lands belonged half to the Liberian government, half to the American Colonization Society – that is, to U.S. citizens. Diplomatic traffic with France, through Grover Cleveland's ministry in Paris, ensued.

The French then signed a commercial treaty with the notorious African slave-trading chief, Samory, and pretended it was a land treaty. This diplomatic sleight of hand also affected Liberia's borders – to the north, this time. French forces won the day against Samory – and indirectly against Liberia. As the century wore on, more Liberian territory was later lost to both France and Britain: indeed, Liberia might never have survived at all without the diplomatic crutch of Washington.

Despite setbacks, the U.S. remained active in Africa's Indian Ocean after the Civil War. *Merikani* – hard, American-made white calico – had been a trade staple on Africa's eastern coast for the first two thirds of the century. During the Civil War, European firms produced *merikani* (calico still has the same name in ki-Swahili) and with the introduction of steamships and the opening of the Suez Canal were able to undercut American prices when American ships returned to the area in the late Sixties. East Africa's main export to New England at this time was gum copal, used in varnishes.

As part of slave trade repression, Britain appointed a vice-admiralty court on Zanzibar under Consul John Kirk, an explorer in his own right, in the 1860's. Kirk was prejudiced against 'people in trade' – although they were virtually the only serious reason for any foreign power's official presence in Africa. Like most nineteenth century Britons, he was especially biased against Americans. Consequently, his relations with Consul Francis R. Webb, who was both a businessman and an American, were never good. Secretary of State Hamilton Fish instructed Webb, however, in 1872, to advise the Sultan to accept some British proposals aimed at cutting down slaving by the Sultan's subjects.

The U.S.S. *Yantic*, under Commander Byron Wilson, arrived at Zanzibar the following January. On Webb's instructions, the consular interpreter altered Commander Wilson's words so that he appeared to be urging the Sultan to stand firm against Britain. When an ultimatum arrived from Sir Bartle Frere in the Cape, threatening Zanzibar with bombardment, Webb's successor advised the Sultan to concede.

With the American inventions of kerosene and the hurricane lamp, U.S. trade revived slightly: but the empire-building Kirk, who had become the *éminence grise* of the Sultan, over-shadowed the Yankee merchants. A sly intriguer, Kirk discredited the Americans at every opportunity. His successor, Evan Smith, appears to have been no more scrupulous. Soon, Anglo-German imperial rule in the area drove the Sultan into puppet power, and eliminated American and other non-British, non-German trading houses.

30

To the north, in the early Seventies, the Khedive Ismael employed about thirty Americans among the experts helping to modernize Egypt. The Americans were mostly military instructors, some of them serving officers on authorized leaves of absence. The two senior men were retired U.S. brigadiers, one unionist, one confederate. (They followed in the distinguished steps of George Bethune English of Massachusetts, a marine from Harvard, who became an Egyptian general under Mohammed Ali and helped destroy the Mamelukes in the campaign of 1820–21. He and two other officers from the United States converted, at least nominally, to Islam.)

The Khedive's campaign of the Seventies pressed into Ethiopia, where Surgeon-Major Thomas D. Johnson of Tennessee was wounded and captured, then saved from execution by an Ethiopian nobleman. The *Ras* obtained a long audience with the Emperor Johannes for Major Johnson, who took a letter from the *Negus* to Queen Victoria. Under the American officers, the Egyptian army appears to have re-established the Khedive's command over all his traditional domains. Officers like Lieutenant-Colonel Mason, Colonel Henry G. Prout, Major Erasmus Purdy and Brigadier Raleigh Colston made long mapping expeditions deep into the Sudan.

The site of today's Aswan Dam was originally selected for that purpose by an American army engineer on secondment, Major Oscar Eugene Fechet of Michigan. Ex-Confederate Major William P. A. Campbell, a noted Arabist, was with Gordon at Khartum, where he died of cholera. Gordon's chief of staff, Colonel Charles Chaillé-Long, was from the eastern shore of Maryland but had fought for the Union. His *My Life in Four Continents* makes stirring reading, particularly his account of his mission from the Khedive to King M'tesa of Uganda. The surveyor of Lake Albert was Alexander McComb Mason, a Confederate graduate of Annapolis. Thus, unofficial American diplomacy, here as elsewhere, preceded a more official contact.

Late nineteenth century American explorers in Africa include Thomas Stevens of the *New York World* who – after going around the world on a bicycle, and riding an unbroken horse across the Russian empire – crossed a broad swath of Africa to join Stanley on his way back from the Emin expedition. Both correspondents were soon overtaken by Frank

Vizetelly of the *Herald*. In the Nineties, Somalia and Ethiopia were explored by the millionaire sportsman-physician, A. Donaldson Smith. Earlier, in 1884, U.S. Navy lieutenant Mason A. Shufeldt became probably the first foreign explorer to cross Madagascar – the world's second largest island. He made the trek on foot, taking with him across the war-wracked territory five hundred *pistoleros*, presumably at the Navy's expense. The spirit that animated most of these men, as Clendenen and Duignan have pointed out, was principally sheer adventure – usually with a dash of idealism.

Americans who flocked to points farther south, at the turn of the century, were mostly of a less altruistic breed. Here, gold was the spur. Many of the travelers were fugitives or 'remittance men'. But investors back in New York were destined to play a bigger role than the individual 'shovel and bucket' prospectors, engineers and farmers. At Kimberley, the American Ethelbert Woodford became the 'town engineer' in 1876, and later tried but failed to win official American support for the *boers* in their war with England.

Farther north, another American, Adam Renders, was reputedly the first white man since Portuguese times to 'discover' the ruins of Zimbabwe. Renders, by then, had become something of a legend: he had abandoned his family and 'lived native' as an elephant hunter – becoming perhaps the prototype for Edgar Rice Burroughs' idealistic Tarzan.

PART TWO
1884–1935
From Bismarck to Ras Tafari

Berlin and After

It was in 1869, in Paris, that James Gordon Bennett, the owner of the *New York Herald*, instructed Henry Morton Stanley to find Dr David Livingstone in Africa. The far-flung reporter, who had covered the Napier invasion of Ethiopia the previous year, reached Zanzibar in January, 1871. Marching a thousand miles, with the Stars and Stripes at the head of an impressive column, he reached Livingstone's *boma* at Ujiji ten months later.

In 1873, Stanley was in the Gold Coast with Lord Wolseley, covering the second Ashanti War for the *Herald*. In 1874, he set off again for Africa to discover the source of the Congo – the 999-day trek that produced his most famous book, *Through the Dark Continent*. The journey was backed by the London *Daily Telegraph* publisher, Edward Levy-Lawson, whose request to Bennett to share the crushing expenses of the trip drew the superbly laconic telegram: 'Yes. Bennett.'

This incredible journey stirred the world's imagination: but it particularly aroused the ambitions of King Leopold of the Belgians, then financially advised by Henry Shelton Sanford – former American Minister in Brussels, who had resigned from the diplomatic service to help the monarch's money grow. Sanford became the delegate of the English-speaking countries in the 'Association for the Exploration and Civilization of

Central Africa', formed in 1876. The following year, Leopold sent him to Marseille to meet Stanley on his arrival from the Congo journey. Sometimes referred to as 'General' Sanford (he was an honorary militia major-general in Minnesota), the big, bluff, wealthy and ostentatious diplomat was a commanding figure at the Berlin Conference of December, 1884 to February, 1885.

It was in 1879 that Stanley agreed to return to the Congo in behalf of an international group sponsored by Leopold, with Sanford in a prominent role. New York interests were in the hands of John H. B. Latrobe, president of the American Colonization Society, founders of Liberia. Stanley departed with an American assistant, Sparhawk, once again provoking rumors that the United States sought imperial expansion in Africa. What finally pushed Leopold to be more assertive were the activities in the area of Savorgnan da Brazza, in behalf of France. French colonies were particularly protectionist and exclusivistic, and a French presence south of what is today Brazzaville would – Belgians, Germans and Americans all feared – be a dead hand on an area of vast potential commercial wealth. Britain, meanwhile, combined with its ally Portugal to keep the French encroachments down.

President Chester A. Arthur in his annual message to Congress in December 1883, gave strong moral support to the International African Association and its American chief executive, Stanley. In April 1884, the Secretary of State, Frederick T. Frelinghuysen, as a result of judicious lobbying on the Hill by Sanford, ordered U.S. officers to 'recognize the flag of the International Association as that of a friendly government'. The French and Germans followed suit in recognizing the I.A.A., and Leopold became the head of the Congo Free State. The following year, the U.S. cautiously agreed, with reservations, to attend the Berlin Conference. This meeting largely mapped out the territories of Portugal, Britain and France in Africa, and established the new claims of the meeting's main proponents, Belgium and Germany.

The U.S. representative at the Conference was to be John Adams Kasson, American Minister in Berlin. He selected Sanford as his diplomatic counselor and asked Stanley to be available to brief the American delegation at every step. The third delegation member, W. P. Tisdale, the first consular

34

officer to be appointed to the Free State, soon quarreled with Sanford and Stanley, who found him stuffy.

As chief U.S. delegate at Berlin, Kasson's instructions were to fight for free trade in the Congo, and to have the Congo basin defined as widely as was possible – against the competing Portuguese and British and the commercial 'dead hand' of the French.

Kasson was to loom large at Berlin, and he has a profound niche in African history. The dour, rangy Iowan was of an Ulster Scottish-Irish Presbyterian family, in America since 1722. He himself had been born and had gone to college in Vermont; he had practised law in Saint Louis before settling in Des Moines, where he had a distinguished Republican party career in the State Assembly and later as a Congressman. He held the post of Assistant Postmaster-General under Lincoln. He was President Hayes' Minister in Vienna in the late Seventies, then returned to Congress. Under President Arthur, he gave up his seat on the Fourth of July, 1884, when he was already sixtytwo, and became Minister to Berlin. He succeeded peppery Aaron A. Sargent, who had crossed swords with Bismarck and had finally been recalled home by Frelinghuysen.

On his way to take up his post in August, Kasson had stayed with Minister James Russell Lowell in London and later with Minister Nicholas Fish – son of former State Secretary Hamilton Fish – in Brussels. Fish presented Kasson to Leopold, and the Iowan spent the following night at the Belgian château of Sanford, then away in London with Henry Stanley.

By 1883, the International African Association, founded in Brussels in 1878, had become the International Association of the Congo – in fact had become an exclusively Belgian body in all but name. Meanwhile, Stanley had signed numerous treaties with chiefs and established twentytwo I.A.A. stations in the western Congo. As early as June 1881, Sanford, alarmed at Portuguese pretensions at the Congo's mouth, had urged State Secretary Blaine to appoint a consul on the Congo, whose salary the I.A.A. would gladly pay.

In Washington, in 1883, Sanford had won over Arthur and Frelinghuysen to his scheme to have the U.S. help redress the power balance in Africa by recognizing the I.A.A. stations on the Congo. The American Colonization Society would be encouraged to believe that the Congo scheme was largely humanitarian and would give it support, Sanford (correctly) estimated. Negro emigration to the Congo would be encouraged. The river basin would absorb U.S. trade expansion and strike a blow for free trade against the French in the heart of Africa. John Tyler Morgan, a blustering ex-Confederate brigadier from Alabama, then chairman of the Senate Foreign Relations Committee, was won over also to this Republican plan. He saw the Congo as a place in which to encourage settlement by emancipated slaves, and as a market for Alabama cottons.

Willard Tisdale, the third U.S. delegate in Berlin, was a Democratic nominee of Morgan's who had achieved fame as an explorer of the Amazon. After his initial quarrels with his colleagues, he was sent off to open his consulate on the Congo, without attending more than the opening shots in the conference.

In February, 1884, Britain signed a treaty with Portugal recognizing Portuguese claims to the river mouth. (Modern Cabinda is a relic of Portuguese claims.) The United States then recognized the I.A.A.'s authority in the Congo valley. Paris, preferring Leopold to Lisbon and London, followed suit. Bismarck also backed Leopold. By adding American weight to the Brussels–Berlin–Paris axis, the U.S. was for the first time intervening in the power politics of Europe. At the conference, Kasson spoke up publicly for humanitarian policies, winning a reputation for *naïveté*. He left Stanley and especially Sanford to deal with territorial and political matters, in the wings.

The fourteen-nation sessions opened November 15, 1884 and lasted three months. Bismarck was friendly to John Kasson from the start, recognizing his enthusiastic identification with empire-building. Kasson reported that German–American relations were now 'altogether amicable and agreeable'. The chief American delegate pushed, as expected, for a wider definition of the Congo basin, to include the watershed of the great lakes of East Africa, with freedom of trade and 'neutralization' of the area. In this he was fairly successful, despite French and Portuguese opposition. To fortify neutralization, Kasson proposed that the signatory powers outlaw war by the mandatory submission of all disputes to an international court of arbitration. Finally, the principle of peaceful intervention by a mutually acceptable third party was agreed.

Sanford, as agent for Leopold and for a Belgian consortium that wanted to build the railroad between the Congo's upper and lower courses, sought a monopoly for this project; here, Kasson prudently dissociated the United States from delegate Sanford's 'private' proposal, and this bid was in fact rejected. The wisdom of having put Sanford on the official delegation was soon to come under fire in Washington: the Democrats came to power that month for the first time since the Civil War – hunkering for issues to discredit the last administration.

Kasson proposed that the natives' rights to 'dispose freely of themselves and their hereditary territory' be respected, and that 'spirituous liquors' be prohibited. (He had supported Prohibition in the United States.) Both proposals were rejected. Prohibition would have meant the searching of vessels, which all the other mercantile powers opposed. Britain proposed that the nations should eradicate slaving (the work of the Arabs in the Congo) and Kasson amended this to make the final form of the wording stronger: Abolition became the 'duty' of the nations.

At the beginning of the conference, Germany, Italy and Spain had sent naval vessels to the Congo, to forestall the Portuguese. On Kasson's advice, Frelinghuysen got the Department of the Navy to send Admiral Earl English, commander of the European squadron, there as well, to seek a 'healthful point well situated for a commercial resort [through] a concession from the natives [providing] a depot and factorial establishment [for U.S. traders]'. By then, Parliament in London had refused to ratify the Portuguese treaty on the Estuary, and Britain decided to back the I.A.A. and free trade after all. English, however, found no 'healthful' resort along the Congo river; disillusionment was soon to set in as it became clear that Kasson had been deceived – particularly by Sanford – about the 'international' and 'humanitarian' nature of the Congo Free State.

In the November, 1884 election, the Democrat Grover Cleveland had defeated Blaine, making Kasson's ministry in Berlin a pin feather on a lame duck administration – and ensuring an early end to direct support by Washington for European imperial growth. Rising Congressional and public criticism of the U.S. role in Berlin followed. The Berlin Conference had been the first occasion on which the U.S. had participated in an international meeting considering territorial matters out-side the western hemisphere. There had been, of course, strong isolationist opposition, led by Congressman Perry Belmont, from the start. It was notably suggested by opponents of Kasson's attitude at Berlin that U.S. approval for international freedom of navigation on the Congo might lead to pressures for giving a similar status to the Mississipi.

Kasson fought hard in his despatches for American support for the Berlin agreement: but Cleveland's Secretary of State, Thomas F. Bayard, bluntly opposed the United States becoming entangled in European alliances – thereby losing the trading advantages which Kasson's diplomacy had obtained. Ageing and disappointed, Kasson returned to Washington in 1885 to lobby for the Congo treaty which he had signed.

On August 1, 1885, Leopold wrote to President Cleveland to inform him of the change of name of the Association to 'Independent State of the Congo', and asking that the recognition of the I.A.A. be extended to the successor state. 'The union between Belgium and that State will be exclusively personal', said the new central African potentate in Brussels. In his instructional letter of September 11 to Minister Tree in the Belgian capital, Secretary Bayard made the point that Kasson and Sanford should not have signed at Berlin, as they 'did not have plenipotentiary powers'. Back in Washington, Kasson correctly pointed out that no multilateral convention is binding until ratified by the home governments. Kasson had support from the maverick Democrat Morgan and sympathy from former Secretary of State Hamilton Fish: but Fish advised Kasson that Sanford's presence in the U.S. delegation had been a mistake. Bayard, in his brief to Tree, held out hope, however, that the United States might recognize the independent state of the Congo – which it became the first power to do, the following month.

Before long, the horrors of Leopold's rule in the Congo made Congressmen glad that they had withheld ratification of the Berlin treaty, and the United States joined in general pressure from the great powers that led to Leopold transforming his African estate into a colony, under control of the Brussels parliament.

Stanley made a final journey to Africa in 1887 to rescue the

German, Emin Pasha. In 1892, he resumed British citizenship, apparently lured home by the offer of a knighthood. He became an obscure backbencher in parliament: at his death, his last request – to be buried next to Livingstone in Westminster Abbey – was refused by the Dean, on the grounds of the explorer's insignificance.

U.S. missionaries were soon active in the Congo, in Livingstone's – and Sanford's and Kasson's – wake. The first great figure was a Negro pastor, William H. Sheppard, who made a deep and risky penetration of the interior to establish his post at Luebo. A second conference on Congolese and African affairs was held in Brussels in 1890, the American delegation being led by the irrepressible Sanford. Shortly after, in 1892, a memorable explorer-figure, Richard Dorsey Mohun, became a much-traveled incumbent of the office of commercial agent in in Kinshasa (the name that preceded and followed Léopold-ville). In warfare with the Arab slavers in the Ngaliema and Kivu regions, he fought as an officer in the Belgian-led Free State forces, becoming *ad interim* commander of an expedition on the upper Congo. He was later promoted Consul in Zanzibar. In retirement, he returned to the Katangan region of the Congo as a mineral prospector and businessman.

For many years, America continued to take a lively interest in the affairs of the Congo, trying to ensure free trade and opposing the liquor traffic. In January, 1908, the State Department bestirred itself over rising reports of cruelty and oppression in Leopold's vast domains: Secretary Elihu Root instructed Minister Henry Lane Wilson in Brussels to take a firm line with the Belgians. Wilson replied that the Belgian parliament was already anxious to take over the Congo from the King and had been pressing for this for the past twelve months. The British Minister in Brussels, Sir Arthur Hardinge, initially urged delay in any Anglo-American joint pressures: but finally Britain's Foreign Secretary, Sir Edward Grey, was won over to the State Department's activist view.

Wilson pushed for a speedy takeover of the King's domains and for reforms 'satisfactory to international opinion and public opinion in the United States'. The Belgian official view, despite the Berlin convention, was that the taking over of the Congo from the King was not an international concern. The United States and Britain pressed for 'absolute freedom of commerce, the rights of Christian missionaries, humane and equitable treatment for the native population'. The United States laid extra stress on the latter point, opposing excessive taxation, forced labor and land seizures. Finally, an annexation treaty acceptable to the Brussels parliament was hammered out, offering a huge indemnity to the King.

In March, Consul-General James A. Smith in Boma reported colorfully and extensively on the cruel situation in Ituri, where workers were being kidnaped and sent in neck chains to work on the Kindu railroad or in the goldmines and rubber forests. There was 'no general administration,' he noted: the state treated the natives as 'negligible quantities'.

In Brussels, both Hardinge and Wilson harassed the reluctant Belgian authorities throughout the year. Both London and Washington were basically anxious for improved trading, land buying and missionary rights – agreed to under the Berlin convention and other treaties that Leopold's administration had failed to respect.

The 'Colonial Law' was passed by the Brussels parliament in August and by the Senate the following month. On October 31, the King created a colonial ministry. But by late November, the new American Consul-General in Boma, William V. Handley, was reporting further exactions, quoting from British Consul Wilfrid Thesiger (later the noted Arabist) who had just 'spent four months in the interior'.

In January, Secretary Root was writing to the Belgian Minister in Washington, stressing the rights of 'native sovereigns' who had signed Stanley's treaties. This squalid page in the Congo's tortured history was slow to turn.

The Wild South

At the Washington level, Africa was still seen, principally, as being 'distant'; but when the Portuguese authorities, prodded by *boer* interests, seized the property of the Delagoa railroad in 1889, Grover Cleveland reacted angrily. The owner of the railroad (from Lourenço Marques to the Transvaal) was an American, Colonel Edward McMurdo, who had sunk his fortune into the enterprise. This appears to have been the first major American investment in the continent.

Boer-fed Portuguese fears of British expansionism lay behind the Lisbon seizure. McMurdo's chief engineer was an Englishman, Sir Thomas Tancred. The following year, a Swiss arbitration tribunal found for McMurdo on all points: Portugal had to pay a large indemnity.

The more idealistic, individualistic American presence remained as well, notably in the missions that were scattered across the continent: these now included many Negro missions, notably those of the African Methodist Episcopalian Church. It was American missionaries who translated the Bible and prayerbooks into Zulu. Others spread into Portuguese Africa. The Protestant missions in Angola and Mozambique, opposing officialdom in a way that the official Catholic church could only rarely afford to do, was to become a potent factor for reform: Protestants developed an 'educational' resistance to the repressive style of government that persisted and persists in the Portuguese territories.

Missionaries also settled in Rhodesia, encouraged, curiously enough, by Cecil Rhodes, the leader of an imperial *mafiiosi* which had nothing to hope for from Christian teaching but condemnation. Rhodes, the swashbuckling son of a British pastor, cynically saw their presence as 'reducing humanitarian criticism of the company in Britain'. (Rhodes' company had a charter to govern the colony.) In Nyasaland, one product of an English mission, John Chilembwe, studied in the United States and returned to establish a Protestant mission of his own, aided by Negro American missionaries. He was to lead a brave but premature and unsuccessful revolt against imperial rule in 1915.

By the end of the nineteenth century, there was a profusion of part-time U.S. consular offices in newly booming South Africa. The legendary Gardner Fred Williams was for a while the consular agent in Kimberley. With the 'Jameson raid' and the approach of the *boer* war, there were attempts to draft Americans into *boer* service, while pro-British American settlers like David Robertson were arrested by the local authorities for 'treason' (Robertson was acquitted but expelled.)

A career consulate was set up in Pretoria in 1899. With war approaching, identification documents became compulsory. On October 11, Consul Charles E. Macrum asked the Secretary of State what papers he should issue to Americans. The next day, as his British colleagues packed their bags hastily, he took over British interests. The British had made a bad mistake. Macrum absorbed all the *boer* prejudices: his empassioned despatches espoused their cause, sometimes with the unwitting humor of the humorless. He passed on, unchecked, numerous *boer* complaints, such as British soldiers firing on the Red Cross flag or misusing a flag of truce.

He was also apparently traversing a personal crisis. On November 6, 8, 11 and 18 he sent cables – each confirmed by letter – urgently requesting home leave, and saying mysteriously that he would 'explain why' on arrival. By the 22nd, he is acknowledging the Department's refusal of leave, and reporting that the British are unloading neutral ships (including, presumably, American ships) at Cape ports.

He again applied for leave, telling the Department there were 'other matters of intense public interest that I hope to be able to lay before you personally'. If this were not possible, he would, he added cryptically, have to 'present them in the form of despatches when the opportunity arises'.

When the *boers* sought to impress Americans into the police, Macrum protested that such service should be voluntary: but he then encouraged Americans to volunteer.

The appeals for leave resumed, concluding with the words: 'I will forfeit the post if the Department doesn't approve on explanation. Please reply.' Assistant Secretary David Hill interpreted this as an *offer* to resign and scribbled a recommendation of acceptance on Macrum's cable. The Vice-Consul was put in charge temporarily, and Consul W. Stanley Hollis was drafted in from Lourenço Marques. He turned out to be equally pro-*boer*, as did a frequent Consulate visitor, *Washington Post* correspondent David Easton. Already by January 5, 1900, Hollis was writing fulsome praise of the sturdy *boers*, the 'sincerity' of their religion and the 'superiority' of their intelligence over that of the Europeans back in Europe. Both Hollis and Macrum seem to have identified the *boer* struggle to establish a white man's rule of the gun with the American revolution. There was the same frontier religion, the same unsympathetic British with their unsuitable European ideas. The native population of South Africa replaced, in the minds of the two Americans, the unspeakable Red Indians. African kings were comparable to Geronimo and Sitting Bull, in an age when no white man doubted that Custer was a hero. Even *boer* censorship of diplomatic traffic did not put them off.

Most private Americans in South Africa, however, sided with London, no doubt partially for linguistic reasons; a prominent exception was a West Pointer, Colonel John Y. Fillmore Blake, who commanded a pro-*boer* unit of Americans – mostly fanatically anti-British Irish-Americans.

John Hayes Hammond and Gardner Fred Williams, two American engineers, had played a prominent role in Cecil Rhodes' bid to overthrow *boer* control. They had claimed the support of five hundred American settlers in Johannesburg and throughout the Transvaal. The failure of the premature 'Jameson raid' dashed their plans. Hammond was arrested and sentenced to death, but finally bought his life with a massive fine. Another American adventurer who participated in the plot was Morris B. Heany, who died in Southern Rhodesia in 1928.

Colonel Adelbert S. Hay arrived in Pretoria in February 1900, and presented his letters to the *boer* authorities of the South African Republic. He, like Macrum, was still representing Britain: but beyond conveying mail and tobacco to British prisoners of war, he confessed that he was not sure what he was supposed to do. The emotional reporting from Pretoria had shifted official U.S. sentiment toward the *boers*, but neutrality prevailed as an overt policy.

On March 10, May passed on the South African Republic's plea for U.S. intervention to procure a peace: but this request for mediation was declined. The British captured Pretoria. In June, Hay died. Consular Agent William D. Gordon took over and was soon reporting bitterly on the high *boer* death rate in the British concentration camps.

On October 1, the State Department cabled the death of President McKinley; but the cable failed to arrive and it was not until the confirming letter was delivered on December 3 that Acting Consul Gordon was officially informed. He complained testily. On June 3, 1902, the *boers* finally surrendered.

Consul Joseph E. Proffitt, who replaced Hay, rapidly took up discrimination cases against Negro American settlers who suffered such indignities as being forced off the sidewalks, obliged to travel third class in trains and forbidden to indulge in trade: but Proffitt met with no success. Under the British occupation, race laws were eased; but the new laws were not enforced and local white conduct remained unreformed. One American was convicted for possessing liquor. Proffitt also reported on the successful adaptation to the cold Transvaal climate of imported Texan cattle.

A light note enters the post's reporting under Proffitt's successor, John Snodgrass, who sent home a *Rand Daily Mail* clipping on August 23, 1905: this reported that the 'Sultan of Zula' in 'Eritrea' had proposed to Alice Roosevelt, the President's daughter, who had 'taken the offer under advisement'. Snodgrass reported 'resentment' in the American community about the report.

A large segment of the American community attracted to South Africa in its get-rich-quick era were similar to the riff-raff that had spread out through the western United States a decade or so earlier. Even the consular service was not exempt: Snodgrass's predecessor, Proffitt, went into business locally and was soon in trouble, running up debts and writing rubber checks. He was reported by the Consulate to have swindled an illiterate and impoverished American called Abraham Moses Saba (presumably a black) out of life savings. Creditors seized property of Proffitt's – some of which turned out to be goods left in consular custody by Americans who had fled at the outbreak of war. Snodgrass was drummed out of a local club because of Proffitt's unpaid debts to the organization. Later that year, Vice-Consul Henry J. Meyer resigned, implicated in a wartime scandal over stores that had come to light. Snodgrass defended Meyer as unjustly accused: this seems unlikely in the light of his resignation, and inevitably casts suspicion on Snodgrass also. (The Vice-Consuls were all part-timers, engaged in business.) But with the peace, Snodgrass got Consul-General rank, in order to be equal in status to nearly all his colleagues. He at once petitioned hopefully for a new typewriter, explaining at length the efforts that had been expended on repairing the only one the Consulate-General then possessed.

· · · · ·

44

American interest in South Africa stemmed in part from Henry Stanley's dynamic view of the continent as a place for settlement and especially investment. During the colonial period, South Africa and its immediate neighbors seemed the most promising African areas for exploitation. Teddy Roosevelt's hunting trips also brought American interest to South and East Africa. The Anglo-American Corporation of South Africa started in 1917 and was initially the largest single U.S. interest in the area; but it soon lost all but a fraction of its American participation; for decades now, it has been an Anglo-South African company with a deceptive name.

In 1929, Cape Town Consul-General Ralph J. Totten was to become the first American Minister in South Africa, bringing the number of U.S. legations on the continent to four (after Monrovia, Addis Ababa and Cairo). This followed a South African request of the previous year, sent through the British ambassador in Washington. Totten moved to Pretoria in 1930. At the end of 1929, South Africa sent Eric H. Louw – later a foreign minister – to Washington. South Africa, by this time, was taking over half America's exports to Africa – $52,864,813 worth out of $94,813,132.

A Consular Case Study: Peter Strickland of Gorée-Dakar

As free trade bloomed in southern Africa, it withered on the Atlantic littoral, despite the obdurate efforts of some testy Coasters. A particularly interesting figure – and a typical case study – of this period was Peter Strickland, a Boston merchant. He represented trading houses in west Africa and persuaded the State Department to make him Consul on Gorée, the island which protected the fishing village of N'Dakarou – now Dakar. He was to prove an unusually thorough and readable reporter of trade and political conditions. He weathered ill health and tragedy with fortitude, and his story had an ending of subtle defeat to challenge fiction.

On September 20, 1883, Strickland, then 46, wrote from

45

Dorchester what became the first letter of the 'Gorée–Dakar' file, now in the National Archives. He had been asked to select a spot in northwest Africa, and wrote that 'Gorée-Dakar would be the best location for a Consulate at present, both on account of its mail facilities and because the other Consulates are there'. He noted that Messageries Maritimes mail steamers left Dakar for France on the 5th and 20th of each month. The State Department agreed to his choice, and on October 6 Strickland wrote back accepting the official offer of the post.

Strickland's early despatches report on the navigability of local rivers, population size and the volume of trade. Senegal was then importing over one million dollars a year of U.S. goods, but only about one fifth of this quantity was freighted in American bottoms.

Like many of the other U.S. Consuls in Africa, Strickland fought off a suggestion that his post be downgraded to a Vice-Consulate, pointing out that his colleagues all had Consul rank. Since his services were free, the bureaucracy's reasons remain obscure – but the altercation was typical of the period and of the end-effects of recurring isolationist demands in Congress.

The submarine cable from the Canaries reached Saint-Louis in December, 1884. From Saint-Louis, there was a land line to Dakar. Strickland reported the Dakar–Saint Louis railroad as near completion. Trade, meanwhile, was quiet, and the following year Strickland applied to go on leave, leaving his Vice-Consul, a Frenchman, and his own son George in charge. But the Vice-Consul fell ill and had to be sent home – only to die, on the Fourth of July, on board ship.

The Department denied Strickland leave, opposed his request (the first of many) for funds to defray his consular expenses – while still restricting his business travel. His fees from consular work were apparently minimal. He suggested two possible names for a new Vice-Consul, and the Department preferred the American candidate – his son. George, then twentyone, was appointed, and Strickland made arrangements to bring the rest of the family out from Dorchester on a visit. That year a submarine cable was completed to the Cabo Verdes.

In 1886, Strickland reported warfare upriver, and the French capture of Ziguinchor, now the capital of Casamance, from the Portuguese. The British began to pursue their cable line from

Dakar toward Bathurst, Freetown and Accra. Inland in Senegal, violent resistance to the French advance continued all through the year, and affected trade. Strickland also reported the German takeover of the formerly American rum trade: 'The capacity of the unrectified African to absorb into his nature this kind of 'rectified' spirit is something phenomenal,' noted the dour Yankee.

In 1887 came the telephone line between Dakar and Gorée. In July, Strickland finally departed on leave, using a permission granted nearly two years before – and pointedly enclosing a certificate from the *médecin-major* 'advising' the Consul not to come back before December. The French doctor diagnosed 'tropical anemia with frequent bilious states and congestions of the liver'. Strickland sailed for Boston, via Bordeaux.

While he was away, the U.S. Minister in Monrovia, Charles H. J. Taylor, came up the coast to trans-ship for home. Regulations were that passengers coming from yellow fever zones must stay in quarantine, in Dakar, before reshipping; but in practice direct trans-shipment without touching shore was generally permitted. Taylor was refused trans-shipment and treated rudely: it seems certain that what he encountered was the usual French merchant marine reaction to a black face, especially a sophisticated one. George Strickland dived into the ensuing diplomatic rumpus with distinction, writing detailed and carefully worded complaints and reports in both languages. He youthfully begins his first affidavit (in French): 'I, the undersigned, George Strickland, aged 23 1/2 . . .'.

Strickland Senior returned in time to witness the administrative separation of Dakar and Gorée. Shortly after, George set off for Saint-Louis, about eighty nautical miles away, on the American schooner *M. E. Higgins* and fell overboard during the night. A ship's boat failed to find him. Strickland had brought George's nineteen-year-old sister back to Gorée with him from Dorchester; but father and daughter both returned home to console Mrs Strickland the following year.

George was replaced as Vice-Consul by René Potin, a Gorean – presumably a Eurafrican. The older Strickland, pleading once again for an annual salary of one thousand dollars, plus 'perhaps an allowance of $300 for office rent', stressed the future potential of Dakar, which was now 'a new city of elegant buildings, wide streets shaded with trees and a large park'.

47

Strickland had recently suffered financial loss when his main commercial employer had gone into liquidation.

Potin was more fortunate. Taken on as agent by a Boston merchant at one hundred dollars a month, he began to spend more and more time at Bissau and soon resigned. Strickland had hoped to go to Europe for his health in 1889, and in 1890 he asked for leave in Dorchester, suggesting that the Consulate be closed and left in the charge of a Cabo Verdian caretaker. Strickland began a search for a consular agent for Saint-Louis, later reporting that he could find no one prepared to do the job without pay. One suspects that he was understandably trying to make a point for himself. In December, however, he recommended Francis Lawton, agent of a Portland, Maine, company for the job, and Lawton was finally appointed. Strickland went to Europe and America, leaving Lawton in temporary charge at Gorée.

The next year, Strickland reported his belief that the French intended making Dakar a major military and naval station. Later that year, an impressive naval battery was mounted on the high cliffs of Gorée island. Growing French ambitions had to be paid for by greater French commercial profits. French taxes soon began to hit American goods: trade at Dakar and Saint-Louis declined. Then, in 1893, cholera struck. By 1896, Strickland, no doubt badly affected by the fall-off in trade, was still pleading for his stipend of a thousand dollars to help support his family back in Massachusetts. The following year he went home and was seriously ill, returning to Gorée at the end of the year. In 1898, he again vainly raised the salary question. In 1900, yellow fever befell Senegal, keeping many ships away. Strickland's daughter was among the victims. In July, they both went to France for two months' convalescence.

By now, Strickland was sixtythree and beginning to worry about the survival of his west African career. In 1901, as part of his plea for a subsidy, he sent a photograph of his big house and consular office on Gorée, partly overlooking the sea on the ocean side, near the island's only beach and jetty. The picture is extant in the files. That year and in 1902, he had authorization to go on leave but could not afford it. Pleas for compensation became more frequent. In 1903, Dakar became the capital of French northwest Africa – as Strickland had earlier predicted it would – ousting Saint-Louis.

That year, he sailed for home via Liverpool and was asked to weigh moving from Gorée to Dakar. He said office rent in Dakar would be fifteen hundred dollars a year, against not much more than half of that sum on Gorée. Given the global and American living costs of the time, French Africa's were clearly already vertiginous. The other consuls, he argued, were still on the island. Britain had a career man, a former army officer whom Strickland said the French regarded as a spy – although what he was meant to spy on is not made clear. The French must have been even more suspicious in 1904, when the Russian Baltic fleet arrived at Dakar.

The next year, with the rains approaching, Strickland began to give up hope. He decided with apparent Department con-concurrence to close the Consulate down 'temporarily'. The archives, including those of Bathurst – transferred to Gorée in 1900 – were to be sent down the Coast to Freetown. He sold his own representational agency to a French firm. On July 21, eleven days before his sixtyeighth birthday, he closed the mission.

This apparently caused misgivings in the Department. On May 5 the following year, State wrote to Strickland at Gorée, apparently forgetting that he was in Massachusetts. The letter was sent on to him. It offered him twice what he had asked for, for so long: he could have two thousand dollars a year. Although nearly sixtynine, he expressed a willingness to return if his continued receipt of funds from his French mercantile successors (perhaps a *rente viagère* which could not be converted into cash) did not conflict with what was required of a salaried consul. At least, he said, he was anxious to put the Consulate back into shape again, instead of it being without a house or furniture, its files scattered to Sierra Leone, before handing over. Apparently his *rente* was an insuperable barrier under the regulations. J. W. Johnson was appointed in his place in 1907, but seems not to have taken up his post. By then, U.S. representation north of the Congo river was reduced to two posts – the Legation at Monrovia, and the Freetown Consulate. (Dakar was to reopen in 1915, when the Freetown mission was closed down and merged with it.)

Madagascar: the Case of the Murdered Consul

The United States had made its consular presence in Tamatave, the southern port of Madagascar, permanent in the Eighteen Fifties. There were U.S. consular agents dotted all around the vast island – mostly, but not all of them, American. Despatches sent to State from Madagascar in the nineteenth century were so voluminous as to be worth a monograph of their own.

Since the French defeat in 1815, the Indian Ocean had been essentially an Anglo-American and Portuguese sphere of influence. In 1881, Washington ratified a treaty of peace, friendship and commerce with the Queen, Ranavalona III, negotiated by her prime minister, Rainilaiarivony. This succeeded a consular treaty, also drafted by Rainilaiarivony, in 1867. In 1882, both the French and British attempted limited colonial takeovers. The French were to prove more persistent. In 1885, in the wake of the Berlin Conference, France signed a treaty with Ranavalona, but soon found pretexts to send in troops again.

On March 4, 1887, John P. Campbell took up the U.S. Consulate in Tamatave. French troops had been in the port earlier that year and had just withdrawn. Campbell's first despatch recounted that the Hova flag of the Queen had just been raised over the little city again. Campbell received his *ex-equatur* from the Queen's governor. He was also presented with a bullock, six chickens and two geese – gifts from the Queen and the prime minister.

Campbell was a rum-swilling, sycophantic bureaucrat. The strongest American figure in Madagascar at the time was one of his consular agents – Captain Victor F. W. Stanwood, whose office was at Andakabe and whose sector was the West Coast, along the Mozambique Channel.

The vigorous Stanwood and the hesitant Campbell quarreled frequently in their polite, measured correspondence. Stanwood recommended to State (over Campbell's head) that the Consulate be moved up to Antanarivo, the royal capital. Campbell successfully resisted this with several pages of arguments, notably mentioning the fact that the three largest American firms in Madagascar all had their main offices in Tamatave. At the time, Antanarivo, two hundred miles away, was separated from Tamatave by 'eight or ten days on men's shoulders', Campbell wrote.

Campbell also sought to belittle Stanwood with State, reporting rumors that Stanwood's mettlesome personality was a frequent source of disputes on the West Coast, and suggesting that he be replaced. Word of this presumably reached Stanwood, for we find him writing Campbell later that year (1887) to warn him that rumors were circulating about his drinking habits. Campbell took the thinly veiled threat as a useful hint and thereafter spoke reasonably well of Stanwood in his despatches to Washington.

Stanwood, who wrote clear, detailed despatches in excellent handwriting, got deeply involved in efforts to stop slave-trading. He also reported often on the fighting in his area caused by a feud between the governors of Andakabe and Inahabo. Several times in 1887, Stanwood told Campbell he was receiving death threats from British Indians involved in the slave trade. One report sent to Tamatave on August 20 said that 'those slavers will probably attempt to kill me or burn my house or both'. On February 17, 1888, he noted in another missive that for six months he had been 'compelled to keep firearms within reach night and day for safety's sake'. There had by then been several other murders of foreigners.

Finally, a despatch on December 9 that year, from an acting consular agent in Andakabe, reported that Captain Stanwood had been shot and killed: but he had been the victim, not of slavers or of some agent of the hostile French but of a Mauritian-born schooner master, Captain du Vergé, who claimed U.S. citizenship.

Stanwood had gone to the little port of Belo, following the shipwreck of du Vergé's Boston-registered *Solitaire*, which had been driven shoreward by currents and curtly refused assistance by a French warship. The schooner was refloatable, but the trading rights of du Vergé, a dubious character, were unclear, so – to prevent him leaving – the Hova authorities had dismasted his ship. Stanwood had arrived at the house where du Vergé was staying to find a violent quarrel going on. When he intervened, du Vergé drew a gun and began to fire recklessly, mortally wounding his own brother-in-law and Stanwood. Agent Stanwood thus became the first U.S. foreign service officer to die from violence in Africa.

In 1896, the U.S. viewed with reserve the French takeover of Madagascar. In Tamatave, Consul Edward Telfair Wetter took a firm line with the French Resident, Ferraud, as did his British colleague. The French agreed to maintain the 1881 treaty terms: but they soon excluded all except the French entrepreneurs from mining. After angry exchanges, the U.S. finally recognized the French Resident-General in August.

Ethiopia: Mission to Menelik

Another kingdom was to fare better than Madagascar. Washington had virtually ignored the Italian invasion of Ethiopia in 1895, and the historic Ethiopian victory at Adowa. But the ancient empire's continued independence was finally to make its point in U.S. diplomacy.

At the turn of the century, a distinguished American diplomat noted in a letter to the President that an area of Africa had 'remained the one spot on the globe where a powerful government exercizes authority over some millions of subjects recognized as free and independent and [whose government] has absolutely no point of contact with our own.'

The diplomat was Consul-General Robert Peet Skinner in Marseille, who had suggested to President McKinley in 1900 that a mission be sent to Ethiopia, the tri-millennial domain of the King of Kings. In 1903, McKinley's successor Roosevelt commissioned Skinner to make the trip.

Skinner left Marseille on October 25, arriving at Jibuti November 17: he and his party proceeded to Dire Dawa by rail. Then the American group – Commissioner Skinner, a surgeon, a Commission secretary, a courier, a marine captain, a naval lieutenant, twentytwo marines and a male nurse – pressed on by camel and mule to Addis Ababa, leaving Dire Dawa on November 29 and reaching the new Ethiopian capital on December 18.

A royal escort of three thousand brightly dressed men at arms, on foot and on gaily caparisoned horses, came out of the city to meet them. Skinner wrote: 'They were picked men, riding well, their *shammas* flying in the wind'.

The visitors, who drew huge crowds of onlookers, were impressed by Menelik's roadbuilding inside the city, and by the picturesque *tukul* architecture of the eagle-eyrie capital. They were at once led to the Emperor, through courtyards stacked with Italian weapons, captured at Adowa eight years before. They were saluted by an honor guard, under a Swiss officer.

Menelik received the party surrounded by his officers and ministers. He wore a cape and headcloth, diamond ear drops and finger rings. The Greek court secretary, Sourvis, interpreted the Emperor's remarks into French. The monarch spoke only Amharic: but he swiftly made a favorable impression on the visitors, whom he held in conversation, with 'two thousand spectators looking on with undisguised curiosity'.

The Americans left the audience chamber to a twentyone-gun salute from the captured cannon, and the playing of 'Hail, Columbia'. The Ethiopians seemed genuinely pleased that the U.S. had no imperial ambitions and sought only to foster trade. Skinner estimated Ethiopia's foreign commerce at the time at $2,316,000, of which $1,389,600 was with the U.S. This included Ethiopia's import of $579,000 worth of *merikani* and the American purchase of $675,000 of skins and $135,100 of moka (coffee). In his final report, Skinner was to recommend the creation of an American shipping line to Jibuti, and the posting of an American trading representative in the country.

After the royal reception, minstrels and officials led the Americans to the palace of *Ras* Waldo Giorghis – an uncle of the Emperor – where they were to stay. *Ras* Waldo lived on his estates and was not in the city at the time.

The following day, a negotiating session began at ten o'clock. Skinner had come prepared with a commercial treaty written in Amharic by Professor Littman of Princeton, who had not been to Ethiopia. Menelik was suitably amazed. At the conversations, the French advisor Léon Chefneux interpreted. Chefneux and the Swiss Alfred Ilg were then the most powerful foreigners in the country, Skinner noted in his later report.

Skinner found that Menelik was not without cognizance of world affairs: Reuter telegrams were received in Aden, typed, and sent each week by boat to Jibuti, whence they went by train to Dire Dawa, where they were translated into French and sent on by courier to the Emperor, the more important items being telephoned from Dire Dawa. Skinner found English widespread, despite the almost total absence of English traders. (Indian traders may have been responsible for introducing English as a trading language.) There were, however, 'hundreds of Frenchmen scattered throughout the country', and French was then the accepted foreign language of the Court. Addis Ababa, according to Skinner, then had about fifty thousand inhabitants, including two hundred Europeans.

The talks went on daily, and Menelik, who absorbed information like a blotter, was interested in Teddy Roosevelt's hunting safaris in Africa. He left the visitors in no doubt of his thirst for modernization.

The mission made the diplomatic rounds and drank Turkish style coffee with the *abuna* of the official Coptic church, an Egyptian. Captain Sir John L. Harrington, the dean of the diplomatic corps, who had been there since 1896, was away. The acting dean was Major Ciccodicola, who had managed to cure the post-Adowa enmity against Italy and was building a telegraph line from Addis Ababa to Massawa. The French minister, Léon Lagarde, was an area specialist, having formerly been Governor of French Somalia. The biggest embassy, Skinner found, was the Russian one. The Czar had given Addis Ababa a free hospital, staffed with Russian doctors and nurses. But, the Commissioner noted, 'our Russian friends have no apparent stake in Ethiopia . . . There are no Russians in Ethiopia other than official Russians'.

The party had Christmas dinner with the British *chargé*, Clerk, who served turkey and plum pudding. The resident corps, Clerk admitted, was puzzled by the American mission. Skinner wrote that 'the role of the various Legations in Addis Ababa is political. The American mission was the only one based upon purely commercial considerations which Menelik had received up to the date of our arrival'. Ethiopia was then cut off from the sea by the Italians in Eritrea and Somalia, and by the English and the French in Somalia also. To the north and west lay Egypt and the Sudan, where the British were predominant. U.S. trade would be dependent on the French railroad.

Menelik expressed an interest in sending Ethiopians to American schools and colleges. 'Yes, our young men must be educated,' Skinner quotes him as saying. And the Emperor added with a self-confidence rare in the Africa of his time: 'We are a very primitive people'.

Before the Americans departed, Menelik gave a huge banquet. The Emperor ate apart, but a cover was laid before a symbolic empty chair at the head of the American table. The servants 'tested' the wine by drinking a few drops of each bottle, from their palms. The visitors were served European food, but tasted some of the Ethiopian food prepared for the Emperor. Skinner noted that 'these dishes are invariably seasoned with some sort of concentrated fire which seemed to race through the system and scarify the whole alimentary tract'. The party enjoyed thirteen courses, and toasted the Emperor and Roosevelt in champagne; as twelve hundred more guests filed in to eat the great feast of leftovers, there was music. For this multitude, *tej* (Ethiopian mead) was served from a pump.

Skinner described Menelik as combining the intelligence of a Bismarck with the 'faculty of handling men by sheer amiability of a McKinley'. He was noted by all, said Skinner, for his tendencies toward 'conciliation and kindness'.

Gifts were exchanged before the mission's departure: Menelik was chiefly taken with a hunting gun, which he tested on the spot, firing through an open doorway at an outer wall – after Horatio Wales, the Commission secretary, had given a similar demonstration. Menelik was amused at blank cartridges, which he had never heard of before; he asked for some with which to test the courage of his officers by pretending to shoot at targets balanced on their shoulders. Before Skinner and his men set off for the coast, Menelik visited *Ras* Waldo's palace on a 'brightly caparisoned mule' and inspected the tented marine camp there.

Menelik sent back to Roosevelt, with the party, two eight-foot elephant tusks, weighing three eighths of a ton between them, and two eight-month old lions. The officers each received a sword, buckler and two lances. All the party were decorated, and Menelik did not forget two medals for two marines who had been sent back from Dire Dawa, sick. (All the decorations were later handed in to the State Department, in accordance with law.)

Because of the presence of the lions, the American party

55

could not get mules. Forced to use camels, they had to avoid the steep mountain trail they had contemplated taking, and return by the route used before. The party took leave of the Emperor on December 27. Léon Chefneux and numerous Ethiopian nobles rode out for several hours with Skinner's troop; Menelik's palace servants brought out jars of *tej* for the final rounds of leave-taking. Both at Addis Ababa and at Dire Dawa, a good deal of nostalgia was expressed by all.

One of the lion cubs died crossing Mount Asabot, and was buried according to Ethiopian rites for domesticated lions, wrapped in a *shamma*, Skinner records. His companion reached the Washington national zoo safely.

Liberia: the Unwanted Offspring

Another independent African state, this time much less sure of its viability, was Liberia. In 1909, the government in Monrovia sent a mission to the United States to ask for help in ensuring the little nation's 'perpetuity'. Native risings and French frontier depredations were again a problem. Booker T. Washington was consulted. The U.S. and Britain both made 'statements of interest', in Liberia's behalf. Secretary Root showed special concern for America's obligations in a letter to President Roosevelt, and persuaded him that a commission should be sent out to Monrovia.

Roosevelt's successor, President Taft, in his instructions to the Commissioners, hinted that they should examine the possibility of officers for the Liberian Frontier Force (L.F.F.) and the customs service being provided by states that were not 'interested' (colonial) countries. At the time, there were British officers in both services – and frontier disputes with the British in Sierra Leone. The United States subsequently decided to lend Liberia money to pay off its international commitments, to appoint a financial advisor who would also be a tax receiver, and to post American officers to the Frontier Force. The U.S. was also to loan a Director of Agriculture.

The next year, financial reforms suggested by the American advisors were approved by Liberia. Britain, France and Germany signaled their approbation. American good offices were used to settle frontier disputes with France and Britain. But the American army officers had still not arrived by January, 1912, when Liberian soldiers were killed in a new frontier conflict with British-officered troops from Sierra Leone. British threats of further strong-arm action followed. Under American advice, the Liberians agreed to a boundary compromise.

On April 11, acting Secretary of State Huntington Wilson informed Ambassador Reid in London that a U.S. military *attaché* and three officers were on their way to Monrovia. They arrived in May. The *attaché* was a serving cavalry captain who was to have the local rank of major: the others were three retired NCO's who would have the rank of captain or lieutenant in the Liberian force. American advisors helped the Liberian government in its continuing dispute with its European creditors. The American-led Frontier Force, aided by bombardment from a U.S. warship, put down bush risings in 1915.

By then the world war that was to affect every aspect of all the great powers' policies had broken out. But for State Department officers concerned with African affairs, 1914 had begun on a lighter note: U.S. Ambassador Walter Hines Page in London had written to Secretary of State John E. Osborne, on February 21, to say that 'Sir E. Grey informs me that a Negro named Sam has been spreading propaganda among the population of Boggs, Oklahoma, and selling shares in an African Trading Company with a view to inducing Negroes to emigrate to the Gold Coast Colony'. Her majesty's government had 'found that Sam's transactions are not genuine', and Grey had pointed out that Gold Coast traditional land law and the climate of the country would make such an emigration 'undesirable'. For several weeks, Ambassador Page was passing on relevant facts in the Sam situation in the best diplomatic tongue-in-cheek manner. But the British government took the whole matter seriously enough to impose a twentyfive pound security deposit on all immigrants to the Gold Coast; it instructed its Vice-Consul in Portland, Maine, not to issue British papers to the steamer *Curityba*, which – said British ambassador Cecil Spring Rice – 'I understand has been

57

purchased by Chief Sam and is the property of the Akim Trading Company of South Dakota'. The end of the year came and went. The *Curityba* sailed, taking Chief Sam to Liberia. But the twentyfive pound deposit law stayed on the Gold Coast statute books until independence two generations later.

Barbary Revisited

At another end of Africa, the problems were more native in origin. Up in the Rif mountains of northern Morocco, in 1904, the brigand chief Thami al-Raisuli set a pattern frequently copied in recent years by activists in Latin America and elsewhere: he kidnaped an American businessman and his stepson in Tangier, and held them to financial and political ransom.

Raisuli required not only fifty thousand dollars in rescue money, but also – a Tupamaro touch – the dismissal of Raisuli's political rival as governor of Tangier, the release of Raisuli's fellow-tribesmen from durance vile (with their place in the cells to be taken by some loyal sheikhs who had opposed Raisuli), the disbandment of the King's whole northern army, and finally recognition by the King that Raisuli was himself the legitimate ruler of four provinces. Teddy Roosevelt proved to be an urban guerrilla's dream: not only did he come up with the ransom money, but by sending seven warships to Tangier he pressured the King into executing Raisuli's other wishes. The two American captives were released.

The King's writ was crumbling, and Moroccan events were moving toward that European interference that the United States had feared for a hundred years. In January, 1908, Mulay Hafid overthrew King Abd el Aziz, and was proclaimed King at Tetuan in June. The European powers and the United States bargained for their recognition of the new monarch, seeking assurances that he would respect the two-year-old treaty of Algeciras (signed April 2, 1900) determining Morocco's relations with the powers. Hafid won general recognition in October, after friction with the foreign communities had led to a massacre of French, Spanish and Italian residents in Casablanca. At the time, all diplomatic agents were still stationed in Tangier, and the U.S. was represented in Casablanca by a Spanish consul.

Farther along the Mediterranean coast, Washington 'took note' of Italy's defeat of Turkey in Libya in 1912. But Washington refused to 'participate in the settlement of political questions which are entirely European in their scope', as Secretary P. C. Knox put it the following year to the French envoy, Jusserand, when the French obtained a protectorate treaty in Morocco. Knox also insisted that the Franco-Moroccan treaty was insufficiently detailed about the King's former treaty arrangements to be fit for submission to the U.S. Senate. Broadly speaking, European colonization of the African territories was seen in Washington as posing more problems than it solved. At the outbreak of the world war in 1914, Britain exchanged recognition of the French protectorate in Morocco for French recognition of a British protectorate over Egypt – captured from Turkey: but the U.S. continued to hold out for the internationalization of Tangier.

Washington was by now having trouble with the French takeover of Morocco. Until November, 1915, Paris was trying to issue *ex-equaturs* in behalf of the 'Sultan' of Morocco inside that country's Spanish zone, and in the proposed international zone around Tangier. (The French had 'demoted' the King from his original title.) Officially, though, the U.S. had come to terms with the French takeover.

In 1917, Washington recognized Britain's *de facto* protectorate over Egypt. Hampson Gary, Diplomatic Agent and Consul-General, called on the British High Commissioner in January, 1918, and on the Sultan, Fuad, later. Fuad expressed thanks for the services of American officers in the Egyptian army under his father, the Khedive Ismail. In April, Washington extended formal recognition to British rule.

The Tangier question came up again in 1923. The French objected to the United States having direct relations with the Sultan, and insisted that – since Tangier was a part of the Sharifian empire – the city and everything else in Morocco was a French concern. The French also objected to the Spanish official presence in the country's north.

The main powers still stationed their envoys in Tangier,

with consulates in Casablanca or Rabat. Ambassador Harvey reported from London in October that 'the British government is endeavoring to obtain complete and independent internationalization of Tangier. In opposition, the French will attempt to create a nominal internationalization, really under French control'.

The French then let it be known that they were preparing a proposal giving rights to all the Algeciras powers except Germany and Austria: but later what was produced was a treaty linking only Britain, Spain and France. Portugal and Holland conceded, reluctantly, the loss of capitulatory rights: but under the leadership of Italy and the United States, most of the powers excluded by the new proposed treaty protested.

In a letter to the British, French and Spanish envoys in Washington, Secretary Hughes drew their attention to many anomalies in the new treaty. Portugal joined the U.S. position. But Belgium and Holland adopted a weaker attitude and Sweden decided to accept the Anglo-Franco-Spanish *diktat*. The United States announced that it would not participate in the government of the International Zone, but insisted on an American presence in the mixed courts when cases involving Americans were being heard.

Matters came to a head in June, 1925, when a meeting of the old Tangier 'Sanitary Council' was held, with the U.S. *chargé d'affaires* emphasizing U.S. rights under previous treaties, and the French representative demanding the surrender of the Council's archives and funds. The Belgian and Dutch representatives insisted that they were still awaiting instructions from their governments. Portugal joined America in opposing the three powers, and the Council's Italian chairman refused to hand over the money. France then pushed the Sultan into issuing a *dahir* abolishing the Council.

There followed an angry meeting of the diplomats at the Italian Legation. When the new Zone government was inaugurated, the Italian, Belgian, American and Portuguese ministers boycotted the ceremonies. The following month (July), the U.S. also said that it would not recognize the right of the French and Spanish navies to patrol the Moroccan coast outside territorial waters.

Perhaps the most significant element in the dispute was the

U.S. decision not to share in the Zone's administration. The first world war had threatened to embrace the United States in permanent international commitments: Washington was now withdrawing. The United States did, however, join the International Court in The Hague. The instinctive return to isolationism strongly affected the country's African policies generally.

Elsewhere in that continent, the treaties signed with the Belgians, the French and the British in the early Twenties sought to correct the handicaps imposed on American trade by the failure of the United States to join the League: the treaties gave America the same rights in the mandate territories (former German colonies) as League members – based on America's status as one of the victorious powers. But the treaties were honored more in the breach than in the observance, especially in French Africa, and American trade with the 'dark continent' declined. The French and British frequently imposed import and exchange restrictions in their African colonies in violation of U.S. treaty rights under the Berlin and armistice conventions. But the cost to the U.S. was not great. Also in the Thirties, U.S. protestant missions began encountering persecutions and harassments in Africa from French and Portuguese authorities – notably in Morocco and Mozambique. All in all, it was a period of U.S. retrenchment, partly voluntary, partly resulting from foreign pressures and intimidation.

Liberia: the Light in the Tunnel

The period from the beginning of the first world war to the beginning of the Second was thus marked by a diminution of America's traditional African interests. Trade with the continent revived during the period of the first European conflict, but was soon outdistanced by European industries, aided by colonial protectionism. America's interests in the period were mostly with its protégé Liberia, and to some extent with North

Africa: there were also the beginnings of close links with Ethiopia.

Liberia was still plagued by internal risings. In 1915, the government in Monrovia asked that the U.S. warship *Chester* should remain off the Kru coast to help it deal with unsettled conditions there. But the *Chester* was needed (presumably to protect neutral U.S. shipping in the Atlantic). Washington offered Liberia, instead, cheap arms and ammunition, giving as the pretext for the removal of the *Chester* the difficulty in getting coal in West Africa.

By the New Year, the *Chester* was still in Liberian waters: in February, Minister James L. Curtis suggested that it remain a few weeks longer until the Kru rising could be subdued. The commander of the *Chester* concurred, and a two-week delay after the arrival of the arms was agreed by Navy Secretary Josephus Daniels. The Liberian government's continuing problems with its native population probably reflected the way in which the world war fever had spread to parts of Africa. The improved Frontier Force was needed in too many places at once. Rebel Liberian tribes got arms from Sierra Leonean traders: when these reportedly sent the freighter *Prahsu* to Bettu with guns, Secretary Robert Mansing protested to Ambassador Rice. Britain made inquiries and denied the report.

Liberia's economic problems were as bad as ever, despite occasionally stringent measures. The end of the war in Europe brought no relief. In January 1919, Liberia's President Howard sent Major John H. Anderson, the American commander of the L.F.F., to pacify the Cape Palmas zone. Anderson captured a vast supply of arms and took numerous prisoners, whom he used to build roads to improve future military movement in the district. But by then, Major Anderson was the only remaining U.S. officer. A request was made by the U.S. *chargé d'affaires*, Richard C. Bundy, for the two existing captaincies to be filled at once and for the United States to supply an Interior Commissioner.

The more permanent problems were financial. In 1922, President Warren Harding and Secretary Charles E. Hughes failed in a year-long battle to get Senate approval for a five-million dollar loan to Liberia, although the House passed the measure and the Senate Finance Committee reported it out favorably in June. At the time, arms and equipment for the L.F.F. were badly needed, as well as public works supplies. By May 13, U.S. Minister Solomon Porter Hood was reporting from Monrovia that the Liberian government was behind on army and civil service pay, and was anxious to draw on ten thousand pounds of enemy (German) property funds already theoretically pledged for another loan. He and the American financial advisor authorized use of these German funds: both were quickly reprimanded by Secretary Hughes. An irritated exchange followed, with Washington expressing pained surprise that Liberia's financial records were not in order.

Hood pointed out that the endorsing of the German Liquidation Collateral Plan (G.L.C.P.) did not involve the United States unless the loan agreement became effective. The Senate rose without reaching a loan decision, but in December it returned the issue to committee. Liberia began to look for a private bank loan.

The first real glimmer at the end of the bankruptcy tunnel came in 1924, when rubber millionaire Harvey S. Firestone of Akron, Ohio, was forced to look for new sources of supply. The trigger was a British decision, two years before, to restrict the export of crude rubber from the Empire to sixty per cent of normal supplies. At the time, British colonies produced seventy per cent of world rubber – a proportion roughly equal to U.S. consumption.

Liberia, it was found, could produce better rubber than Malaya. Firestone began negotiations for a plantation, offering the Liberian government extensive employment and an export income, along with enough initial funds to refloat the civil service budget. Firestone was also to build a harbor and procure a five-million dollar loan.

The long and protracted negotiations involved the drafting of three agreements, three times each. Firestone's personal frustrations are reflected in his own communictions, including cables to both the United States and Liberian presidents. Sensitivities were raw: on December 24, 1924, Assistant Secretary of State Harrison drew Firestone's attention to 'the attitude of certain of the Company's representatives in Liberia toward the government and people [there],' The Secretary of State, said Harrison, was anxious to see the company use 'tact and judgment' and to show a 'kindly and understanding attitude'.

The brash methods of big business were something new to Liberia, and the State Department intervened frequently to ease some of the harsher terms of the initial, draft ninetynine-year fixed-term pact, which was to be renewable for a further fifty years.

Sydney De La Rue, the American financial advisor to President King's government in Monrovia, provided useful bargaining points for improving the agreement from Liberia's point of view. On April 30, 1925, Firestone cabled President Coolidge that he was still having difficulties with the negotiation over a loan to Liberia to enable it to pay for the port and other developments which Firestone was undertaking. The Liberians did not want a loan that would indebt them to the rubber company – they wanted a U.S. Government loan. When the point was finally taken that this was not possible, Monrovia wanted a bank loan administered by officials named by the State Department – virtually the only foreign body which Liberia had learned to trust. (When an agreement with Firestone was finally signed, the Department was named as the arbitrator.) Toward the end, Firestone hustled everyone, including President King, with genuine threats of competition; but the Liberians negotiated fairly well. They got their loan from the National City Bank's Financial Corporation of America (F.C.A.) in New York, where agreement on all aspects of the Firestone deal was finally reached in September of 1925.

The definitive ninetynine-year accord called for revision after fifty years, then after ten-year periods: it involved annual rental payment of one million dollars for a million acres, plus a small payment for each acre actually brought under cultivation, along with a one per cent export tax on the rubber, less company public works expenses.

Also in 1925, the U.S. used its good offices to prevent further French frontier raids. Frontier delimitation was undertaken the following year. When Minister Hood left Monrovia in 1926 after a long and embattled period at the Legation, he had the satisfaction of knowing that he had played a significant role in pushing a small and understandably wary country, across an historic watershed, into the development age.

At this time, American political interest in west Africa was

64

marginal, except among members of Marcus Garvey's 'Back to Africa' organization. Commercial interest was greater. U.S. imports from British west Africa alone amounted to a third of annual African imports of about forty million dollars.

In 1928, John Loomis succeeded the remarkable Sydney De La Rue as financial advisor to Liberia. In that year, U.S.–Liberia radio communications were established. But Liberia was soon to encounter other 'communications' problems with the world.

Down the Coast that year, a consulate was created in Lagos, responsible for all British colonies and trust territories in west Africa. Monrovia, however, remained the principal and most challenging post, with a new crisis about to break.

On June 5, 1929, Secretary Stimson instructed Minister Francis in Monrovia to call the Liberian government's urgent attention to alleged contraventions of the 1926 Geneva slavery convention – mainly in regard to the shipment to Fernando Póo of Liberian labor, virtually seized by the Frontier Force, with the active participation of corrupt high government officials.

That week, Francis reported that the Barber Line was worried about accepting one hundred native deck passengers at Cape Palmas for Libreville, as they appeared to be shipping against their will. State told Francis to take the matter up informally with the local government.

Liberia prevaricated. Not all apparent slavery was slavery, officials said. It was pointed out to Francis that road-repair forced labor – a certain number of days' service each year from each villager – was permitted under the constitution. The colonies of the European powers exacted similar service – but it was difficult to see what all this had to do with shipping men out of the country against their will. Liberia offered to accept an investigatory Commission. The U.S. supported this proposal. Meanwhile, the Barber Line announced it would take no more deck passengers for Fernando Póo or Libreville.

Then, in July, Francis died, leaving a fellow black diplomat, Third Secretary Clifton R. Wharton, in charge of the Legation. At this time, an American-born Liberian, Thomas J. R. Faulkner, of Monrovia, published a letter in the Baltimore *Afro-American* detailing charges of forced labor. This increased the international pressure for an inquiry.

65

The Liberian government suggested that the investigating Commission be composed of a Liberian, a Spaniard (Liberia's accomplices in the Fernando Póo trade were of course Spanish) and an American – and stipulated that the American should not be a Garveyite or a sympathizer with that movement. By now the mud had splattered further, and even Firestone was having to deny charges that it employed forced labor.

Liberia naturally asked that there should be no representative of a colonial power (other than Spain, presumably) on the panel: but when Dr Sigvald Meek, a Norwegian jurist, declined to go, he was replaced by Dr Cuthbert Christy, a British tropical medicine expert. Liberia accepted him. The U.S. appointed Dr Charles S. Johnson, a Negro sociologist. Liberia chose ex-President Arthur Barclay. After the fashion of the time, the two blacks selected Christy as their chairman. The investigation began in March, 1930, and carried on until September. The Commission's report was critical of Liberia.

The same year, a yellow fever epidemic broke out in the country and a Rockefeller Foundation technician was shipped in from Lagos to help deal with it. The 'sanitary scandal' having been grafted by colonial European opinion on to the one about slavery, there seemed an imminent threat of foreign intervention: the U.S. helped Liberia ward off this threat, indicating that if there was to be any foreign interference in Liberia's internal affairs it would have to be American – which was what the Liberian government wanted.

The U.S. then began seriously to help Liberia solve its sanitary and perennial financial problems. But U.S.–Liberian cooperation was certainly not all easy going. Liberia complained about the attitude of the Americans sent out to officer the L.F.F. – mostly former N.C.O.'s. The U.S.-appointed financial advisor John Loomis, always an influential figure in State Department thinking on Liberia, asked that West Pointers, 'preferably Negroes', be sent out. Negro West Pointers then totalled one in number. Finally a single white man was appointed – Major George W. Lewis, who had been police chief in Puerto Rico.

Disputes festered on about the application of the recommendations of the Christy Commission, made more fractious by a presidential campaign in Liberia during which there were substantial charges of poll rigging. On May 6, 1931, Minister

Mitchell recommended that Washington recognize the election of Edwin Barclay: but the U.S. withheld recognition pending adequate assurances that the reforms recommended by the League of Nations would be applied. Liberia's inabilities to meet its international financial responsibilities also became an issue again. Most of 1932 was occupied with a proposal to appoint an 'International Committee of Control' in Liberia. The U.S. and other powers continued to withhold recognition of the Barclay election. Minister Mitchell remained at his post, however. Liberia was represented in the United States by a consul-general in Baltimore. The interior of Liberia was wracked, again, by tribal risings.

Secretary Stimson began to lean toward the 'Committee of Control' idea, on the understanding that it would be headed by a Commissioner-General from the United States. The fear of French and British incursions, taking advantage of Liberian weakness and using the various Liberian scandals as a pretext, remained real. An arch-figure of imperialism, Lord Cecil, was then president of an 'International Committee on Liberia', in Geneva. Colonel Lewis (he had since been promoted) resigned his post, discouraged by the inadequate authority allowed to him. All through 1933, a proposed League of Nations 'plan of assistance' continued to face heavy opposition from an independence-minded Liberian government.

In 1934, Liberia rejected the League plan completely – having initially accepted it with reservations that had proved unacceptable to the League. The new Secretary of State in Washington, Cordell Hull, strongly favored the Geneva plan, telling Liberia it was 'fair and workable and . . . amply safeguarding Liberian sovereignty'. On August 28, 1934, Liberia introduced its own plan, and Special Assistant Harry A. McBride recommended to Hull that it be given a 'fair trial'. Hull at once offered Liberia help to make it work, and this finally led to U.S. recognition, in 1935, of Barclay's election.

In 1936, the U.S. effectively blocked a British proposal to mandate Nazi Germany (in compensation for its lost colonies) to take over the government of Liberia. This extraordinary proposal had originated with the pro-Nazi South African premier, General Hertzog, the previous year. Britain apparently saw it as a possible way of appeasing Hitler – at the expense of the Liberians, with whom patience in Geneva was wearing thin.

About this time, Minister Lester A. Walton began at last to report some reforms and progress. Liberia signed a new treaty of friendship, commerce and navigation with the U.S. on August 8, 1938, and a new consular convention the following month. With the approach of war, Liberia also received defense assurances from Washington.

Ethiopia: Mission to Yasu

America's relations with Ethiopia followed a desultory pattern until World War Two. In 1906, there had briefly been a Consul-General in Addis Ababa, followed by a permanent Vice-Consul for the next three years. In 1909, Hoffman Philip arrived as Minister Resident and Consul-General. From 1910 to 1913, he was replaced by a 'Vice-Consul General'. Then American interests were placed in the hands of the British Legation, which had a Consulate-General in Addis Ababa and seven provincial consulates.

This end-result of historically inexplicable, pragmatically meaningless decisions in Washington mirrors well the U.S. Government's weaknesses in foreign affairs at the time – and the State Department's rather unprofessional attitude to Africa. Finally, in 1914, U.S. Consul John Q. Wood arrived to begin negotiations for a treaty of commerce with *Lij* Yasu's foreign minister. This was shortly after Menelik's death, and before the advent of *Ras* Tafari (Haile Selassie) as Regent to Empress Zauditu. Wood thus arrived during a period of crisis and hiatus in Ethiopian affairs.

His treaty was to replace the earlier agreement signed by Consul Skinner for President Theodore Roosevelt with *Lij* Yasu's father, Menelik. Wood sat in council with Yasu's advisors and was finally received by the *Lij* on 6 June. He reported Yasu to be wearing a 'black silk bernous' – apparently an indication of the prince's ill-fated conversion to Islam. Wood found the young ruler cordial but simple.

The Minister of Foreign Affairs, presumably hoping for a bribe, did not turn up for the subsequent treaty-signing session: but he and Wood met on mule-back, later that day, as Wood was on his way to protest to Yasu. Wood managed to get the minister to come to the Consulate and present a formal apology. The treaty-signing was set again for the following day, June 26, in a tent: but when Wood arrived, he faced fresh objections from the King's ministers to the clause saying that the U.S. had twelve months in which to ratify the text. Wood accepted a six-month period and was told to return the following morning. Since he was sick with rheumatism and fever and was anxious to leave the country, he was told he could come 'dressed for the trip, on your mule'.

His report says: 'During the entire night of the 26th, the rain fell incessantly. On the following day, therefore, the roads were in a very bad state and the streams were swollen. It was necessary to ride two hours in a heavy rain, to cross several brooks and ford three streams, to climb four hills before reaching the home of the President of the Council, where it was arranged [that] the treaty should be signed and sealed'.

Once again, the Minister of Foreign Affairs was late, and the Keeper of the Royal Seal had to be sent for and found. Then it was stated that the treaty had to be sealed at the royal residence – then, at Addis Ababa's hot springs. Wood, in pain, and angry when a further delay occurred because the French Minister had called, finally forced everyone to go to Yasu. He reported that he arrived himself 'wet and covered in mud'.

The prince went on taking his cure, but authorized the Keeper to seal the treaty – a straightforward most-favored-nation pact – in a small bedroom where Wood was resting from his exertions. In October, President Wilson wrote to Yasu to inform him of American ratification of the agreement. Wood was sick in Washington, but the British *chargé d'affaires* in Addis Ababa delivered the letter on December 20. Yasu replied cordially on Christmas Eve.

The Department of State, however, forgot to remind President Wilson to proclaim the treaty. Someone discovered the pact by accident, in a drawer, in August, 1920 – by which time the initial four years had expired and the agreement (so far as Ethiopia knew) had been tacitly reconducted. State Secretary Bainbridge Colby wrote to Wilson explaining that the pact had been 'inadvertently placed in the Department's files and buried'.

Early in June, 1920, Standard Oil discovered it had also buried an agreement giving the company a drilling concession in Ethiopia's Harar province, obtained by a subsidiary, the Anglo-American Oil Company, on August 26, 1915. The agreement stipulated that prospection should begin before August 26, 1920, which now did not leave much time. Drilling machinery was rushed to Jibuti. Robert Peet Skinner, now Consul-General in London, wrote to Washington for help in sustaining the company's fast-expiring contract. Fortunately, or so it seemed, the concession company included a brother-in-law of the Empress Zauditu, who had succeeded the now-imprisoned Yasu.

Since 1916, *Ras* Tafari – later, Emperor Haile Selassie – had been Regent, and had repudiated many of Yasu's agreements. Haile Selassie was backing the claims of a British group, the Abyssinian Corporation, and gave this firm a counter-concession. Consul Addison Southard at Aden went to Addis Ababa to see *Ras* Tafari and sort out the confusion – stressing to the Regent that an American company had come a long way in good faith and at great expense. If it were disappointed, he pointed out, this would discourage further American investment.

Finally, Anglo-American got half the province, and the British group the other half. The new agreement was reached 'in two days, a record time for Abyssinia', Southard's despatch notes. But no oil finds and no important mineral discoveries were ever made by the companies. (Oil was finally discovered in Ethiopia in 1972.)

American relations with Ethiopia soon fell into abeyance again, and in 1925 *Ras* Tafari wrote to Coolidge asking that the Legation be reopened. He had earlier written to President Harding, who had died before finding time to reply. Foreign Service Inspector Ralph J. Totten was then sent to Addis Ababa: on his return, in June, 1926, he recommended that a Minister be appointed. By that year, there were already in Ethiopia an American school and hospital, the Anglo-American Oil Company, the American Ethiopia Mica Mines Concession and another U.S. firm, the Arabian Trading Company. American commerce with the country was increasing. *Ras*

Tafari's outward-looking policy also argued for more American attention.

In February, 1927, Coolidge asked Congress for funds to open a Legation on July 1, 1927. Congress refused the appropriations. But Consul Southard, who was by then in Singapore, was recommended for the appointment when Congress resumed. By April, 1928, we find him *en poste*, having called at Aden on his way from the East to pick up the U.S.–Ethiopian diplomatic records.

Southard weaved his way carefully through Anglo-American competition to build a Lake Tsana dam. The political sensitivity of the subject sprang from the fact that the dam could affect irrigation in the Nile Valley – Egypt being under British protection. The British wanted priority for an Aswan Dam proposition. Southard also passed on Ethiopian requests to purchase American arms and to have U.S. military advisors. Washington was cool to this, but a reserve U.S. major, Sydney Forrester Mashbir, wrote to *Ras* Tafari offering his services, and informed State Secretary Nelson Trusler Johnson – who passed the information on to Southard in Addis Ababa. Nothing, however, came of this. 'Addis', the Foreign Service's newest Legation, was beginning to look like a quiet, even boring post. But unbeknownst to anyone in Addis Ababa or Washington, Ethiopia was about to become a center of world attention – in a situation where every country's attitude was to determine its right to respect for a generation.

PART THREE
1935–1946
Warrior Interlude

Ethiopia: the Road to Armageddon

The situation which was to sweep Ethiopia on to the world scene began in 1934. On August 29 that year, Captain F. M. Brady, the acting U.S. military *attaché* in Rome, reported that Italy planned to invade Ethiopia, with army and bombers, in a two-pronged attack, under General Graziani, at the 'first pretext'. Italy, when challenged diplomatically, issued the usual denials. Ambassador Breckinridge Long decided to accept the Italian denials at their 'face value'. When Brady's superior, Colonel J. G. Pillow, returned to Rome, he concurred. But the envoy and the *attaché* were gravely wrong: the young captain's assessment of the worth of the initial information had been rudely right.

Curiously, *chargé d'affaires* W. Perry George, in Addis Ababa, a seasoned career officer, was at first as gullible as Ambassador Long, a wealthy amateur, had been. However, hypothesizing on the 'possibility' of an invasion, he drew up a plus and minus table which leaned in favor of the former – economic development, the repression of local slavery, better communications, more security for colonial frontiers with Ethiopia; Ethiopia would acquire a port and Italy a favorable trade balance. Should an invasion actually take place, George said in what must be one of the classic mispredictions in recent diplomatic annals, there would be no strong patriotic reaction.

On December 6, George reported the famous frontier incident at Wal Wal – a clear Italian provocation, since (as he noted) Wal Wal was a hundred kilometers inside Ethiopia. Italians had prevented the onward march of an Anglo-Ethiopian boundary commission.

The Italians already had secured the tacit support of the French government under Laval. Britain told the Ethiopian government that it did not want to get involved in its disputes with Italy. Many officials in both Britain and France thought in terms of 'completing' the colonization of Africa, unaware that the imperial era was only a decade or so from its demise. The U.S. attitude was less colonial: but the U.S. was almost as obsessed as London and Paris with the desire to appease the 'Axis'. Later, British public opinion was to swing London toward a less pusillanimous attitude, and finally toward moral support for Ethiopia. The U.S. remained largely aloof.

By May 29, 1935, Italy was asking Long if it might expect U.S. support if Rome requested a League mandate over Ethiopia. All three western powers now voiced their opposition. By August, there was something of a united (if rhetorical) front. But Laval felt he had established good personal relations with Mussolini at Locarno in 1934, and wanted to preserve them.

On September 17, Ambassador Long had an interview with Mussolini, by whom he was clearly fascinated. But the Duce, Long's despatch also indicates, gave the American short shrift. War was at hand. On October 4, Italian planes bombed the defenseless city of Adowa, symbol of Italian defeat, including a city hospital with a prominent red cross on the roof. The Ethiopians allowed the Italian population to leave Addis Ababa. The new U.S. *chargé*, Cornelius van H. Engert, was deeply impressed by Ethiopian restraint.

To win the support of the League, the Emperor had also delayed mobilization virtually until war began. The League voted sanctions on arms, on imports from Italy and on certain exports to Italy – along with financial sanctions on the Rome government. The U.S. was of course not a League member but appeared to support the sanctions plan. By and large, U.S. influence, at this watershed of history, was ineffective, even in regard to application of the Kellogg Pact (outlawing war) which the U.S. had supported when it was signed. France began to vacillate and influenced London into support of what became Anglo-French proposals for a settlement. These of course involved territorial concessions and were unacceptable to Ethiopia.

On September 10, *chargé* Engert had reported that the Emperor desired direct U.S. mediation, the U.S. being 'the only absolutely impartial great power'. Urged to do the maximum by Stanley K. Hornbeck, chief of the division of Far East Affairs in the State Department, Cordell Hull had made a fairly strong statement, identifying the U.S. with some new British initiatives in behalf of peace. Hull had reiterated the terms of the Kellogg Pact; but Washington had turned down Addis Ababa's request for U.S. mediation. In Rome, Long had proposed his own solution, highly favorable to Mussolini: Italy was to have all of Haile Selassie's domains except what Long called 'the original Ethiopia'. The Italian portion would include Addis Ababa. Italy, France and Britain (but not the U.S.) were to guarantee the integrity of Ethiopia's remaining portion. Long had thrown in a plan for Germany to receive back some of its African colonies in return for agreeing not to seize Austria and for taking part in European disarmament. He had added, however, that he doubted if his Ethiopian plan would succeed in appeasing Mussolini.

At the September 17 interview, without authorization from Washington, Long had tried out his ideas on the Duce, reporting at length to Hull on the poor reception which they received. Like many others at the time, Long was learning, the hard way, that appeasement was like trying to put out a fire with gasoline. The envoy found the Duce determined. 'He does not want an "out" ... He proposes to go straight ahead, in spite of everybody and against anybody,' Long reported.

Meanwhile, Italy's envoy in Washington had also called on Hull and revived Italy's legendary misinterpretation of the Uccialli Treaty, which he claimed Menelik had violated before Adowa. (The Italian view was that by accepting Rome's offer to act for Ethiopia on request, Menelik had given Rome a protectorate.) From Addis Ababa, Engert wrote to President Roosevelt urging pressure on the Duce. In that letter, which has never been published, Engert drew a distinction between the two central European fascist leaders. Although Hitler might merely resent foreign pressure, Engert suggested, Mussolini would be sensitive to foreign opinion, if expressed with enough firmness. Questioned in 1972, Engert, in retirement, still believed his assessment of thirtyseven years before had been right, and that Roosevelt might well have been able to stop a war – the savage conduct of which with impunity soon helped encourage Hitler to launch the second world war.

When Italy sent in its bombers, the U.S. limited policy to embargoing arms to both sides, thereby helping to consolidate Rome's advantage; but Washington refused an Italian request that car exports to Ethiopia also be placed under embargo. Export permits were however refused for two planes, ostensibly being imported by the 'Ethiopian Red Cross'. Under the incipient war conditions, Standard Vacuum gave up an Ethiopian oil-exploration concession: the Emperor suggested that the U.S. use this withdrawal as a bargaining gesture to Italy, which now opposed virtually all non-Italian investments in Ethiopia. Only on October 4, when Adowa was bombed, did the Italians admit that they had begun an infantry advance, with air cover.

On November 22, Hull received the Italian ambassador again: the envoy complained that the U.S. was hostile to Italy's 'pacification' of Ethiopia. Hull read him a long lesson in neutrality. He reminded him of U.S. aid to Italy in the first world war, of how America had written off seventyfive per cent of the Italian debt – and had even failed to collect the rest.

'I pointed out to the Ambassador,' Hull wrote in his recapitulatory memorandum, 'that the League of Nations organization at Geneva solemnly judged an aggressor in this war, while the U.S. did not; that the Geneva agreement seeks to aid Ethiopia, which the U.S. does not; that the Geneva agreement seeks to embargo all imports from Italy – which this Government does not.' Except for the arms embargo, the U.S. did not support sanctions – having accepted Long's recommendations on this. When a United Press story suggested that the U.S. was collaborating on League sanctions, the Department of State telephoned Embassy counselor Ray Atherton in London to get him to deny it. The U.S. position might have been closer to Britain's if London had had the support of Paris. Britain was hoping for the fall of Laval and his replacement by Edouard Herriot. But by and large, Hull's record on the Ethiopian war was a supine one, and he seems to have been the often naïve victim of tongue-in-cheek *démarches* by the Duce's mission in Washington.

As the war approached Addis Ababa, the U.S. considered withdrawing its Legation and handing over consular work to the British mission – which began distributing gas-masks to both Britons and Americans. Many American missionaries and most of their dependents were evacuated, along with some other U.S. residents, including – according to consular traffic – 'ten indigent Negroes'. American buildings had the Stars and Stripes painted on their roofs, in the hope that this might keep off bombers. There were appeals for Addis Ababa and Dire Dawa to be made open cities, and requests to Cordell Hull that the U.S. associate itself with these appeals. Even on this point, the cautious Secretary instructed Long: 'You may make, on humanitarian grounds, representations similar to but not exceeding those made by your colleagues'. Shortly afterward, the Italians bombed the American Seventh Day Adventist Hospital at Dessie.

For several weeks, the Ethiopians thwarted most of the attacks, despite armament disparity and the terror caused by bombing: but finally poison gas made the difference. As the fall of Addis Ababa approached, the British evacuated the Emperor by warship to the Holy Land, from where he went on to Geneva, then to exile in Britain. There were French official objections to taking him through Jibuti, whence he sailed May 4, 1936; these were ignored.

On May 17, Engert, who had become Minister Resident, correctly predicted that 'pacification' would take some time, and noted that the war was not (as the Italians claimed) already over. The U.S., he advised, should not lift its arms embargo. Hull was anxious to resume 'normal' relations with Italy, but Hornbeck advised that these were of more concern to Rome than Washington: he suggested 'watchful waiting'. In Rome, *chargé* Kirk was arguing for 'liquidation of the measures adopted (by the U.S.) as a neutral'.

The career diplomat in Addis Ababa continued to show informed skepticism about Italian claims to occupation and surveillance of the whole of Ethiopia. (At the liberation, five years later, it was learned that the Italians had never managed to occupy more than certain sections of the country.) Accurate political reporting on this point by Engert was to prove historically significant, because of the moot question of recognition of the conquest.

In mid-June, Engert estimated that forty per cent of Ethiopia was 'not even nominally under Italian control'. Columns of less than one thousand Italians dared not move more than five miles from the capital, he reported. He strongly urged against revocation of President Franklin D. Roosevelt's proclamation (of neutrality) of October 5, 1935, since this would imply acceptance that the war was over – virtual recognition of the annexation. He also reported that the Italians were dealing with all foreign interests in Ethiopia 'in a high-handed manner'.

Wallace Murray, chief of the Division of Near East Affairs, which had inherited Ethiopia, advised Ambassador Bingham in London to discourage the emperor's intention of visiting the United States for fund-raising – a visit which Washington lecturer W. Leo Hansberry was trying to arrange. Murray suggested pointing out that an election campaign was on: Bingham should also 'avoid any discussion of the advisability' of a visit *after* the poll.

President Franklin D. Roosevelt's first two Administrations were weak on foreign policy generally: Hull was the watchdog for a government wholly oriented to recovering from the Depression. A close aide recalls Hull as a 'pretty vague man about everything': his spoonerisms on foreign place-names, repeated over and over again (such as Diboutchy for Jibuti) were a constant source of corridor hilarity in the Department. This vacuum at the top left many ambassadors with a free hand to do anything that did not rock the boat: flattering tyrants abroad fell squarely into this category. Already by May 9, 1936, Ambassador Long was telling Italian reporters that he was convinced that Italian troops had 'completely pacified Ethiopia' – in contradiction with the Department of State's own information from the spot. Long added that his three years in Rome had convinced him of Italy's basic 'need' for colonies: he referred with satisfaction to Ethiopia's agricultural fertility. He stressed friendly Italo-U.S. relations. On his return to the U.S. shortly afterwards, he made similarly un-neutral noises to the Press. In spite of all this, he went on to become an Assistant Secretary of State.

Italy reassigned its Washington envoy that year also. The two new appointments raised the question of whether to accept the Italian king's new title of Emperor of Ethiopia. Under-Secretary William Phillips suggested to the departing Italian ambassador that Umberto be described as 'King of Italy, &c., &c.' or 'King of Italy and its possessions beyond the seas', which could be interpreted in America to mean only Libya, Eritrea and Somalia. Finally, the new American envoy's letters of credence merely referred to the 'King of Italy', while the new Italian envoy's also spoke of Umberto as Emperor of Ethiopia. In an exchange of Notes, it was accepted by Rome that this did not imply American acceptance of the conquest: but Italy had scored a propaganda point. Hull was apparently influenced by reports from the Rome embassy that the Duce would not agree to remove the Ethiopian title from his man's credentials. (Even if this had been true, it would only have meant that the Duce's mission in Washington would have been left in the care of the counselor – normally, at the time, the most effective member of any major Italian mission, the envoys themselves usually being noble, politically appointed cyphers.) However, had it not been for Engert, the American position might have been weaker still.

In Addis Ababa, legations began to reduce their representation to *chargé* level: some consulates closed. The Italian occupation had brought violence and danger to the mountain city: all foreigners had their difficulties with the invaders. Italy used troops to shut diplomatic transmitters down. Engert protested strongly when Italian soldiers violated the U.S. compound: he insisted that Graziani get them out. Graziani said the legations were no longer *lex loci* – presumably because their accreditations were to Haile Selassie, not to Umberto.

The new Roman empire was essentially a grocer's dream, and the occupying force began at once to interfere in the country's commercial practices. This of course annoyed the legations, as it cut across existing legitimate agreements. Protestant missionaries suffered persecution. Engert saw Marshal Badoglio often, addressing him as 'commander in chief' and refusing to use the terms 'viceroy' or 'governor-general'. When he mentioned this issue in despatches, the State Department gave its approval to him on this.

The resourceful American diplomat also convinced the simple Graziani that home governments would presume that Addis Ababa had been the scene of a massacre if all diplomatic transmitters went dead at once. Graziani confessed that he 'hadn't thought of that', and ordered radio facilities restored temporarily. The use of cypher was forbidden, for a while, emphasizing Italian uneasiness that the true military situation might become more widely known.

His Washington instructions put Engert under more pressure to be accommodating to the Italian commanders than his British or even his French colleague. When Engert expressed outrage at a group of Ethiopian patriots being executed near the Legation gates, Hull reprimanded him. 'I note that in your letter to the Marshal [Badoglio] you have stated that you "will not in future tolerate the perpetuation of such horrors at the Legation's doorsteps". The impropriety of such a step should be obvious to you in the absence of any knowledge that the Department concurred in the step you have taken and would be prepared to support you in making any such unenforceable demand'. Receiving these comments in the heat and horror of 'Addis' under the Blackshirts, Engert limited his reaction to removing the Secretary's picture from the wall.

He defended himself discreetly, noting that Badoglio 'had been extremely rude to some of my diplomatic colleagues – notably the French minister – and has treated me comparatively decently only because he realized from the very beginning that I would not permit him to bully me. He is a bluff soldier and quite impervious to diplomatic niceties'.

Engert also dealt curtly with the Italian Governor of Addis Ababa for insisting that riders should dismount, and drivers leave their cars, whenever Graziani passed. He called the demand 'medieval' and unheard of 'in any part of the civilized or uncivilized world'. The Governor withdrew the rule.

In February, 1937, Engert reported 'revolting savagery' by 'undisciplined bands of Black Shirts and laborers armed with rifles, axes or clubs' after an unsuccessful assassination attempt on Graziani. He called it 'unbridled brutality and cowardice', aimed indiscriminately at men, women and children who could not possibly have had any links with the bid to eliminate the newly promoted marshal. Engert's despatch told of 'mass executions' and said the streets were 'lined with corpses'. The

79

burning of houses nearly set fire to the American Legation compound. Engert quoted the French envoy as having had his compound invaded by the soldiery, his servants' huts burned and some of his servants abducted. The French minister had reported to his American colleague that the Italian occupying force had become 'raving maniacs'.

Later an American missionary was attacked in Addis Ababa by an Italian policeman: he and an Englishman who came to his assistance were both arrested. Engert arrived and muscle-minded both men's release. Italians continued to 'run amuck' for the rest of the month, he reported. The American compound began to fill with refugees from neighboring houses burned by the bands of soldiers. Relatives and parents of Legation servants, shot by the invaders, were brought into the compound for burial. The tone of Engert's despatches mounted as he described, daily, fresh scenes of 'despicable cruelty'.

On February 22, he concluded a missive with the words: 'Scenes such a this and many much worse have been going on for four days to impress the natives with the civilizing mission of Fascist Rome'. Marauding bands of Italians even attacked Ethiopians wearing marked Legation uniforms. The American protestant missions continued to suffer from lootings and brutality.

Secretary Hull was still more bothered than moved. 'Such conditions,' he cabled, 'are likely to involve us in embarrassing if not dangerous incidents which are not of any vital concern to this country.' He was reluctant to maintain representation at the Minister level. He suggested Engert go on leave, leaving Morris Hughes, a Vice-Consul who had been posted in from Tokyo, to close the Consulate shortly after.

On the evening of February 24, the Ethiopian refugees left the American compound after assurances for their safety, housing and feeding had been given by the Italian authorities to Minister Engert. A delegation expressed gratitude 'to the United States Government' for 'saving our lives'; but later reports suggested that the Italians had soon betrayed their promises.

In Rome, Ambassador Philips suggested leaving Hughes *en poste* as 'withdrawal of all the American personnel might be looked upon as passing judgment upon a situation regarded here as one of [purely] domestic concern'. On February 27,

Engert cabled, agreeing to leave on March 5 and saying Hughes would leave on March 30. He concluded his despatch on a lighter tone: 'He (Hughes) requests that you inform Macy's, New York, cancel recent order drapes and groceries, also instruct despatch agent ship nothing.'

Hull circulated Rome and Addis Ababa with a statement he intended making regarding the Legation closure. Phillips suggested that the wording 'since there are no present or prospective American business transactions in Ethiopia' be removed, as the words 'might well be regarded as an affront'. Hull concurred.

Britain was asked to take over U.S. interests. Engert's suggestion that a Vice-Consul be sent from Aden to Jibuti to help with the evacuation of Americans was rejected. Finally, no Press statement was issued in Washington on the closing of the U.S. mission, because Phillips reported that Count Ciano – Foreign Minister, and Mussolini's son-in-law – would find it 'embarrassing'.

In his final despatches, Consul Hughes reported that the Italians were systematically decimating the educated population. He left on April 9, accompanied by Vice-Consuls Robert L. Hunter and Adrian B. Colquitt. During 1938, Vice-Consul Chiperfield at Aden and Consul Smith in Nairobi sent reports of continued depredations against U.S. protestant missions in Ethiopia. Ambassador Phillips made representations in Rome: British consuls were kept active in up-country Ethiopia, looking after their own and U.S. missionaries.

In October, Rome's ambassador in Washington, Suvich, decided to return to private business in his native Trieste. *Chargé* Cormelli asked a State Department official if the U.S. would now recognize 'the Empire', failing which he did not think a new Italian ambassador would be appointed. Suvich himself, back in Washington to take his leave, called on Under-Secretary Sumner Welles in November, and was told that Prince Ascánio Colonna would be acceptable as the new Italian envoy – but on the same conditions as before. Hull, the supine reed, was at last beginning to straighten up: Roosevelt had started to turn his regard toward foreign policy. Britain, in contrast, recognized the 'Empire' that month in a desperate piece of Chamberlainian appeasement. As the months to Armageddon rolled on, the Department of State's main reporting from

Africa dealt with continued Italian persecution of American medical missionaries within the conquered territories.

One man in the State Department who *had* recognized Africa as being part of Hitler's Grand Design was Henry Serrano Villard; but little attention, Villard noted, was being given to Africa by the policy planners. Even Ethiopia and Liberia were handled by the European Affairs Office. A State Department (non-Foreign Service) officer, Hugh S. Channing, was the desk officer for Liberia.

Then in 1938, Villard was to recall later, 'we made the greatest real estate deal of all times'. It was in that year that the Near East Office acquired all of Africa except Algeria, South Africa and Madagascar, and gave the Europe office the Balkans in exchange. Villard became Assistant Chief of the Near East Division, in charge of Africa – a post to which he was steered partly because he was the grandson of Henry Lloyd Garrison.

That year, Villard made the shakedown cruise on the new warship *Boise*. His principal port of call was Monrovia, where the visitors went ashore in surf boats. Villard noted the necessity for a port. With this in mind, he surveyed nearby Fisherman's Lake in what were still called 'pontoon planes'. (Villard, a flying buff and the author of a history of aviation, first flew as early as 1912.) In Monrovia, Villard found President Barclay leaning to Germany, which wanted iron ore concessions and offered an air line connection. Villard alerted Pan Am, and the U.S. Bureau of Mines – thus taking the first step that led to the giant Bomi Hills concession. He presented Barclay with a replica of the first (1847) Liberian flag, made from the original bunting, and books by his abolitionist grandfather. The flag was a gift from the Phelps-Stokes Foundation.

Villard's interest in the continent was not, however, matched back in Washington, and certainly not by Cordell Hull. It was to be another, post-Ethiopian element of military history – the North African landings of the Second World War – that was to help to increase the size (and, radically, the importance) of the African Affairs section, and to start the move toward separating 'Africa' from 'Europe' at the Department. Hull, with his hazy knowledge of geography, was to survive into that dynamic era too. The real force in African Affairs, apart from Villard himself, was the energetic Near East Division chief, Wallace Murray.

Washington, Africa and the World War

U.S. foreign policy concerns at the outbreak of the war in Europe in September, 1939, were as follows: the importance of maintaining neutrality, the protection of trade, the repatriation of nationals, and the stockpiling of strategic materials such as rubber, tin and copper. There were lesser concerns, such as a special interest in the fate of European Jews, the efforts to prevent Italy entering Germany's war against America's traditional allies, and – after the defeat of France – the desire to continue relations with Vichy. Africa was principally seen as an extension of two of the main belligerents, Britain and France.

But United States neutrality was already strongly leaning toward those two countries. In October, 1940, Italian warplanes bombed a U.S. mission at Doro in the Anglo-Egyptian Sudan, killing an American doctor and his wife and wounding a missionary couple. In the report which finally reached Washington, it appeared that the missionaries had been in contact with the advancing Italians, explaining their inability to evacuate the mission station. A single-engined biplane had made the attack on the defenseless compound, in which the four were standing, holding out an American flag.

On June 24 that year, Hull had asked Consul Jester in Lagos for 'any information you may be able to obtain in regard to the attitude of the armed forces in French colonial territories toward carrying on the war'. It was clear at that time that only a minority of Frenchmen supported Brigadier de Gaulle's bid to pursue the conflict. Jester reported that the British colonies were trying to keep the French colonies in the war, but that French officers were worried about what would happen to their pay, if they should reject the control of Paris.

The French Governor-General in Brazzaville and the Belgian Governor-General in Léopoldville decided to continue the fight. From Léopoldville, Consul Mallon announced the posting of Pierre Boisson to Dakar, and the almost equally defeatist General Husson to Brazzaville, capital of France's colony Middle Congo. From Lagos, Jester reported discord and disagreement among the various French governors in neighboring territories – all essentially political appointees.

In Brazzaville, Husson, who had strongly opposed the British bid to scuttle the French fleet in North Africa (to prevent the ships falling into Nazi hands) attempted to cultivate the Chad Governor, Félix Eboué, a Negro from French Guyana. British intelligence officers in Léopoldville, under Lt.-Col. Clifford Bagot-Gray, mounted a radio campaign which swiftly won majority French colonial support in Middle Congo to de Gaulle; Husson fled to Léopoldville to save his skin when Eboué came to Brazzaville on General de Gaulle's orders to take over the governor-generalship.

In Washington, however, Hull still valued the link to Vichy, and Mallon was instructed only to call 'informally' on Col. de Larminat, de Gaulle's High Commissioner for Africa, and to 'refrain from any action or statement that would commit this government in any way'.

Communications were hampered by problems of transportation. It still took a month to perform what we would think of today as a 48-hour mission – and perhaps soon, with supersonic transport, as a one-day mission.

In the late summer of 1940, Thomas C. Wasson was selected to be U.S. Consul in Dakar. He was, at the time, Consul in Vigo, Spain. Wasson (who died a few years later from an Israeli sniper's bullet in Jerusalem, where he was then Consul-General) flew hastily from Lisbon by clipper to Bermuda. There the aircraft remained grounded by fog.

In New York, Villard 'put the heat' on the Barber Line to hold departure of its ship. When Wasson's plane finally got off from Bermuda, Villard hurried out to La Guardia with the Consulate codes and other papers. A motorcycle police escort rushed Villard and Wasson to Brooklyn docks. The ship had just cast its moorings but threw lines ashore again and put down a gangplank. It was to be the last ship for Dakar until war's end in 1945.

Two weeks after Wasson's arrival, a Franco-British naval

force attacked Dakar, largely unsuccessfully, because of naval units there which Vichy seemed decided not to allow to sail out of German reach. Consul Wasson bicycled to the harbor-view post office on Boulevard Pinet-Laprade each day with despatches about the crisis.

Having a consular office in 'Vichy Dakar' proved very useful. Wasson was able to reassure an anxious Hull that, contrary to rumor, the German Armistice Commission had not 'taken over' in the city – as it had in Casablanca. Nor was the port becoming a German submarine base. (A report had said the submersibles were being fueled locally by peanut oil.)

By November, Consul Wasson could report that the de Gaulle forces had taken over the Gabun. De Gaulle paid his famous visit to nearby Brazzaville that month.

Meanwhile, the Ethiopian war went on – at the time, the only active contribution in Africa to the war against the Axis. But that summer, Hull's advisor on political relations, James Clement Dunn, turned down a request from Haile Selassie in London for arms for the patriots still fighting the Italians.

In Liberia, the Barclay regime was under increasing criticism. Washington was still concerned because of possible German ambitions to control the country. The U.S.S. *Omaha*, under Rear-Admiral David Lebreton, paid an official visit in the fall. *Chargé* Clifton R. Wharton, now on a second tour of duty in the historic Monrovia Legation, reported Spanish attempts to get air landing rights there (on the route between Fernando Póo and Spanish Sahara): on Washington advice, Wharton urged the Liberian government to turn down the Spanish bid. A PanAm route – Villard's 1938 idea – was discussed instead. This would touch down at Monrovia on its way from New York to Cape Town – via Puerto Rico and Natal, Brazil.

The possibility of having PanAm flying boats had been strongly urged by Firestone, the rubber baron, who had the dynamic support of testy Harry Villard. Firestone was finding wartime shipping unsafe and inadequate; Villard shared his belief that Liberia had strategic importance for both sides. Firestone brought pressure on Juan Trippe, the President of PanAm. In December, Liberia agreed to a shuttle service to Bolama, in Portuguese Guinea, using Sikorsky seaplanes. This put Monrovia at only three days' distance from New York.

Hull objected that the contract excluded competing U.S. lines, but the agreement was finally signed on July 14, 1941.

In June, 1940, meanwhile, Diplomatic Agent and Consul-General Maxwell Blake, in Tangier, reported that Spain had occupied the International Zone, using Moorish troops. The takeover was 'in the name of the Sultan' – lipservice to the protectorate treaty – and was to 'assure the absolute neutrality of Tangier and its Zone in the present circumstances', the Spanish announced.

The Spanish Foreign Minister told Ambassador Weddell in Madrid that the 'former' political status of Tangier – with diplomats accredited to the Sultan – was a 'legal fiction and a monstrosity'. This was the Bogart era, with Vichy ruling in Rabat. Spain was clearly trying to profit from the war to incorporate the Intesnational Zone into 'Spanish Morocco, beginning with the Tangier rural districts.

U.S. representatives reported frequent friction with the Spanish and French authorities. When the Vichy French expelled the British consuls from the 'French' zone – a theoretically illegal act, as they had their *ex-equaturs* from the Moroccan monarch – the U.S. joined the rest of the diplomatic corps in protesting. The U.S. also took over British interests.

Washington was soon to begin economic aid to North Africa, essentially to provide an excuse for preserving the U.S. Consulates as sources of intelligence. In equatorial Africa, the Free French got lend-lease aid, on Churchill's urging, under local supervision by U.S. military and naval observers. Lend-lease aid was also extended, at Britain's request, to Egypt's young King Farouk.

Liberating Axis Africa

Early in 1941, the British thrust into Ethiopia began, strongly supported by the Ethiopian resistance, which had fought on ceaselessly since 1935. From Aden, Consul Clare Timberlake

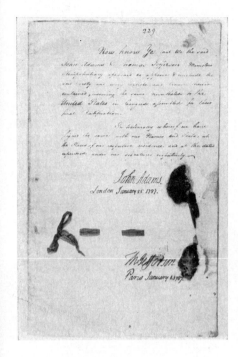

Seal Page, United States–Morocco Friendship Treaty, 1786, signed by John Adams and Thomas Jefferson. Oldest U.S. treaty still in force.

Ceremonial letter from the King of Morocco acknowledging the Instruments of Ratification of the 1786 Treaty by the Continental Congress.

Ratification Instruments of the 1840 Treaty with Zanzibar.

Ceremonial letter from Premier Rainilaiarivony of Madagascar to Consul Waller, 1858.

Seal pages of the 1905 Treaty with Emperor Menelik of Ethiopia in Amharic, French and English, signed by President Theodore Roosevelt.

The first American Embassy in Africa: the Monrovia Legation building, *circa* 1880.

John Adams Kasson

Henry Shelton Sanford

Henry Morton Stanley

U.S. Delegates to the
Berlin Conference,
1884–85.

THE AMERICAN MISSION.

The party in front of its mansion

Consul Skinner's Mission to Addis Ababa

The party leaving the audience chamber

Hofmann Philip

Cornelius van H. Engert

Cordell Hull

Wallace Murray

Emperor Haile Selassie and President Franklin D. Roosevelt

Figures in the Ethiopian Drama

Clifton Wharton

Felix Cole

Clare Timberlake

Henry Serrano Villard

Edmund Gullion

Sheldon Vance

World War Two Diplomats and Envoys to the Congo

Julius Holmes

Edward Korry

Charles Darlington

Authors of Reports

had reported that the Italians had a serious shortage of gasoline – especially avgas. On January 25, Timberlake correctly predicted that the British liberation drive would begin quite soon, and forecast that the Italians would be defeated by the spring.

Sure enough, Addis Ababa fell early in April. Timberlake was authorized to fly in an R.A.F. aircraft to the city, and make reports. The U.S. consular corps still operated on strapped budgets – Timberlake budgeted one hundred and fifty dollars for this displacement. He found the missionary families safe, and recommended a message from Roosevelt to Haile Selassie. The Emperor's own message reached Washington first. On May 20, Roosevelt in reply assured the King of Kings of the 'satisfaction with which I have received these tidings' (of Haile Selassie's return to his capital). Early the following year, a U.S. Consul, E. Talbot Smith, returned to Asmara, although his accreditation remained, for the time being, to the British forces.

In the north of the continent, things had not been going so well. From Algiers, Consul-General Felix Cole had been the first to report, on June 21, 1940, that France had reneged on its promise to Hull not to hand over its fleet to Germany or Italy at the surrender. The news was passed on to Britain, which attacked and sank French ships at Mers-el-Kebir and Oran.

From Casablanca, Consul-General Goold cabled that the French Navy and the civil administration were pro-Vichy, but that a number of army officers wanted an Allied landing in Morocco.

Because of the British blockade of the Mediterranean, there were food shortages in North Africa. French proposals were made to the United States that the British could perhaps be persuaded to allow some small food importations. Free French sympathizers in North Africa were anxious that the population should not become too discontented – for example, from a shortage of green tea, which is mixed with mint for the principal local beverage.

On the advice of the Consulate-General in Casablanca, the State Department recommended the secret resumption of economic aid to North Africa, in the hope of 'subverting' Vichy in the area. Another objective was to keep Socony Vacuum's five hundred Moroccan employees in work, while a further consideration was that Moroccan manganese, cobalt, cork and olive oil would be useful to the United States. Aid – notably food and gasoline – was dropped when Pierre Laval returned to the premiership, then revived in the face of strong U.S. press and Allied opposition. The main channels were through Consul-General Cole in Algiers and Diplomatic Agent White in Tangier; soon a new Consul-General was appointed in Casablanca – H. Earle Russell. To British objections to the traffic, Washington argued that aid would prevent political disintegration, and would strengthen the hand of General Weygand, Vichy's commanding officer, against a German occupation of Tunisia. It might even encourage the French government to move from Vichy to Morocco. Vichy, meanwhile, was protesting the establishment of a U.S. Consulate in Brazzaville, the equatorial African village that had become de Gaulle's capital in Africa.

From 1941, President Roosevelt concentrated his African consular corps in French-speaking North Africa, with Villard as the anchorman in Washington for this intelligence operation. In Algiers, unknown to Weygand, Lt.-Col. Solberg of the Office of Strategic Services was busy planning to bring the French units in North Africa back into the war on the Allied side. Overall chief of the North African operation was Ambassador Robert D. Murphy, who has recounted the saga in his *Diplomat Among Warriors.*

Murphy began his mission by arriving in Algiers on December 18, 1940. He made an immediate call on French Commissioner-General Yves Chatel. From there he went to Dakar where, with Consul Wasson, he held talks with Weygand, an old-fashioned man of honor largely overtaken by events. Murphy and Wasson also called on Pierre Boisson, Vichy's High Commissioner to French West Africa. This archetypically arrogant French colonial administrator – nearly deaf, cranky, irascible, with one leg missing, and the remaining limb in frequent pain – was the almost pluperfect example of the wrong man in the wrong place on the wrong occasion.

Murphy went on to Tunis to see Admiral Esteva. Here, as elsewhere, the French officers unanimously protested that they hoped for a British victory – but said they would do nothing against Pétain's orders. It was hard to know whom, if anyone, to believe or trust.

88

This was the atmosphere for the aid operation that prepared the ground, eventually, for 'Operation Torch' – the Allied invasion of French North Africa. Back in Washington, Hull – sensitive to press criticisms about 'appeasement' following his attitude to Italy's invasion of Ethiopia – never actively supported Roosevelt's economic assistance project. A rising foreign policymaker, Dean Acheson, also was opposed to it.

The project called for the stationing in the area of U.S. observers, ostensibly to prevent the re-export of aid items. In their passports, the naval and army officers were described as 'technical assistants', while the diplomats were categorized as *attachés* of the nearest consular posts. Salaries and expenses were paid from a secret White House fund.

The service officers were sworn in as non-career vice-consuls on April 23, 1941. They were sent off by clipper or ship: one made the trip in a French tanker.

On May 19, Pétain announced closer collaboration with Germany. Hull suspended aid. Two days later, Murphy saw Weygand, who gave assurances that persuaded Murphy to report that the General was 'holding his own in a very difficult position'. Murphy recommended a resumption of aid. If the 'natives' became disturbed and rioted, the Germans would seize the pretext to intervene. Thus, Africa policy was, more than ever, an adjunct of Europe policy: but the war had given Africa a new dimension; fears of African nationalism now helped dictate strategy. The decision to resume assistance was not an easy one for Hull: Britain was, at this point, more reluctant than ever to relax the blockade.

Most of the young O.S.S. 'consuls' in North Africa were soldiers of fortune with linguistic skills. The Germans made extensive reports about all of them. Of Murphy – who had spent a career in consular work until Ambassador William Bullitt recognized his qualities and made him his Embassy counselor in Paris in 1939 – they noted that he was 'of Irish origin' but had been 'educated privately in England'. He was called francophile, sophisticated, a patron of the arts, 'able to deal with any situation'. Although married with three daughters, said the German report, Murphy 'seeks his erotic adventures in his own class of society, without however disdaining a little governess or chambermaid if she be blond, attractive and clean.'

The German political officer clearly had a strong taste for fiction, and perhaps a gift for lending his own personality to his characters.

Of J. Rives Childs, they said he was the 'incarnation of the American businessman'. Although 'born in a wealthy family, and therefore badly brought up, he is a credit to the class which he represents.' Childs was however dismissed as talkative, indiscreet and 'inquisitive'. The Germans said he liked to be called 'Excellency'. They concluded: 'He is incompetent, and may be considered absolutely harmless in his post at Tangier.'

Of the others, the German report noted: 'Since all their thoughts are centered on their social, sexual or culinary interests, petty quarrels and jealousy are daily incidents with them. Altogether they represent a perfect picture of the races and characters in that savage conglomeration called the United States of America . . . The motto "Each for himself and God for all" has never been more faithfully followed than by them.

'We can only congratulate ourselves on the selection of this group of enemy agents who will give us no trouble. As they are totally lacking in method, organization and discipline, the danger presented by their arrival in North Africa can be considered nil . . . We are kept aware of their slightest movements.' The report is now marked in the records 'Received at Casablanca from Ritz, March 12, 1942. R.D.M.' The German diplomatic code having been cracked some months before, Murphy was able to pass it on to Murray as an enclosure to a letter, two days later. Volumes of later German messages also found their way to Washington.

The report's only kind words had been for Consul-General Cole and Agent King. Captain David Wooster King was by then 48. He had served in the French Army, 1914–17, beginning with the Foreign Legion, and had lost an eye in 1915. His life had taken him to places like Ethiopia and the Khyber Pass. He spoke fluent French and some Hindi – a relic of running a burlap business in Calcutta for four years.

King had performed numerous secret missions overseas for the United States. He was described in U.S. records as the 'mainstay of the military and naval intelligence work in Casablanca'. His 1946 Order of Merit citation notes that he set up a clandestine radio station at Casablanca, in contact with Tangier and Gibraltar. It adds: 'When the American

Consulate-General and annex (in Casablanca) were surrounded by French *gardes mobiles*, he made his way through the French lines at great risk to his life, to the Consulate-General, and before capture warned the Consul-General to burn all secret War and State Department codes.' Villard's first pencilled notes, however, found that King was 'not witty' and was an 'unreliable reporter', but admitted that he 'gets along with the French'. Villard ordered: 'Consular superior to check reports'.

U.S. plans to enter North Africa in force at the end of 1942 inevitably strained relations with Laval – who finally severed links with Washington on November 8. With U.S. entry into the war, the previous December, North Africa had become a key area in Army plans. On September 22, 1942, Roosevelt had made Murphy civilian head of General Dwight Eisenhower's operations in the area. He was henceforth always referred to as the 'President's personal representative'. His main task had a new name – 'psychological warfare'. The U.S. invasion was to be presented as guarding the area for France – keeping out the Germans and Italians. Roosevelt told Murphy that 'no change in the existing French civil administration is contemplated by the United States'. No Gaullist forces were to be employed in the invasion.

Secrecy was at a maximum. Murphy revealed in a War College lecture in 1954 that Roosevelt had forbidden him to say anything to the State Department about 'Operation Torch' because 'the Department's security is like a sieve'. It was a time for clandestine meetings with General Henri Giraud, his principal aide General Charles Mast, Colonel Chrétien – the head of French army intelligence in North Africa – and members of the 'Robin Hood' resistance group. With 100,000 German troops massed on the Tunisian border, the French now feared a German invasion from there or from Spanish Morocco.

Admiral Darlan, anxious to save his skin, offered cooperation to the Americans. Cole favored using Darlan, but the French patriots resisted this. A secret rendezvous between Eisenhower, Giraud and Mast took place in Gibraltar, to which the French officers were brough by submarine and flying boat – but not before a prior meeting, in a wine cellar at Cherchell, in Algeria, had been disturbed by a police raid. The French officers had slipped away, just in time, leaving only the villa's owner, along with Bob Murphy, two Consulate-General officers, General

Mark Clark, some other British and American officers and diplomat Julius Holmes, then a colonel.

Murphy, the consular officers and the owner of the villa were pretending to play poker when the French police cars drove up. The police were told that a black market transaction was in progress and there 'might' be a scandal if it was reported. General Clark, whose tales tended to improve each time he told them, said afterward that he had been uncertain whether to shoot the police officers or try to bribe them.

The boats taking the party out to the submarine a few hours later had trouble with the ranging surf: Clark lost some of his clothes and $18,000 worth of gold. But 'the mission had brought back complete plans of all the French military installations in North Africa, the disposition of friendly, dependable troops' and details of airfields for landings, Murphy wrote later.

Giraud unrealistically wanted to lead the planned American invasion of North Africa. His attitude incited the Americans to enlist Darlan's aid after all. On October 20, the admiral arrived in Algiers on his way to Dakar. His son, Alain, had preceded him, to go to an Algiers hospital for a sudden attack of poliomyelitis. General Alphonse Juin, Darlan's overall North African commander, asked Cole for American help in treating polio: Cole passed this request to Admiral Ross T. McIntyre, the White House physician. (Roosevelt, of course, was also a polio case.)

By then, Britain had occupied Madagascar, and handed it over to de Gaulle – but not before independentist sentiments had exhibited themselves in the vast island. Britain now eyed Dakar. In both cases, the Free French resented not being able to deal, themselves, with the Vichyites; but the U.S. was anxious to placate French conservatives and welcomed the British initiatives. Neither London nor Washington was quite sure what sort of France would emerge from the war, or whether Frenchmen would give de Gaulle any place in it.

The Cherchell Conference on 'Operation Torch' had taken place on October 22. The arrangements for Darlan's support fell through. The American invasion of North Africa began on November 7. Pétain ordered resistance, but this was brief. The Germans fought longer, in Tunisia. In Dakar, Boisson closed the U.S. Consulate. In Tangier, *chargé* Rives Childs reported that the Sultan had issued a proclamation, clearly inspired by the French, urging Moroccans to help Frenchmen repel American invaders.

On November 8, Vichy French military police in Algiers arrested Murphy and Vice-Consul Kenneth Pendar. But by then, the invasion was proceeding briskly: they were soon released. 'Vichy' resistance collapsed.

Darlan had arranged to be in North Africa at the opportune moment. U.S. forces took the surrender from Darlan, who went on radio to urge the French in North Africa to accept it. Bloodshed had been largely avoided, and Washington felt its 'Vichy' strategy had paid. But in London the Free French were furious at Darlan's eleventh-hour participation in events. On November 17, 1942, Churchill cabled Roosevelt, advising against 'making terms with local Quislings' and noting that Darlan had 'an odious record'. But on November 22, Mark Clark accepted Darlan as High Commissioner of 'French Africa'. This committed Boisson and other diehard Vichyites to support the Allies. Boisson, to whom Villard had sent a hearing aid, now got the message: he lifted the incommunicado against the American Consulate in Dakar. (The hearing aid gift had been the idea of 'Wild Bill' Donovan, the head of the new, often ineffective 'Office of Strategic Services' – forerunner of the more professional C.I.A.) But Consul Flexer reported that the the 'germanophile' General Falvy, commander in chief of French West Africa, was still making public statements opposing 'the British and above all the Gaullists'. Boisson made no changes in appointments, leaving his conversion to the Allied cause unconvincing.

A full Consul-General was soon appointed to Dakar; a mission under Admiral William A. Glassford arrived to develop Dakar harbor, and nearby Wakam airport, as way-stations for U.S. forces. A similar development was undertaken at Pointe-Noire in French Equatorial Africa. A major logjam was removed when Darlan was assassinated in Algiers on Christmas Day. General Giraud was swiftly appointed in his place.

Meanwhile, down in Aden that month, Consul Timberlake was bringing about the surrender of Jibuti. Earlier, a thousand French and five thousand Senegalese troops had crossed into British Somaliland and Eritrea to join the Allies. On December

28, Jibuti's capitulation was achieved without a shot.
The new administration preferred to liaise with the neighboring British forces, rather than with the Free French commanders, because of lingering anti-de Gaulle sentiments. The
Vichy officials who had held the principal military and civil
roles in the territory during the war were made prisoners.

War's Effects

The war had brought change to Liberia also. In 1942, a full
defense agreement with the U.S. had been signed, leading to
the creation of Roberts Field, a big facility for land planes.
Negotiations began for replacing sterling by the dollar.

In January, 1943, on his way home from the Casablanca
conference with Churchill, Roosevelt had visited Liberia –
refueling at Bathurst, in the Gambia, on the way. He thus
became the first American President in office to visit Africa.
In Monrovia, *chargé* Frederick P. Hibberd had Roosevelt,
President Barclay and Secretary Stimson to lunch at Roberts
Field. Liberia requested and got lend-lease aid for the Liberian
Frontier Force, and other assistance. It was a time of new
American awakenings, and sudden generosities.

President Barclay brought President-elect William V. S.
Tubman with him on a visit to Washington shortly after.
Hibberd noted that Tubman was 'less inspired by color prejudices' than Barclay. Both the visitors, Villard recorded,
bargained hard for development aid.

Roosevelt had a habit of taking action in foreign affairs with-
out informing the State Department. In Morocco, he had assured
Al Glawi, the Pasha of Marrakesh, that the U.S. would back
postwar independence for the Maghreb. Later, U.S. Consulate-
General officers in Tangier were to be surprised when the
Pasha took this up with them. White House memos apprising
State of presidential actions frequently took the Department by
surprise.

94

Some of F.D.R.'s ideas backfired. In 1943, Jonathan Daniels, a White House aide, told Villard that the President wanted a group of Negro journalists to tour French, Belgian, British and Portuguese African colonies. Villard was told that Roosevelt hoped that experience with colonial inequities would help encourage patience among Negroes in their growing demands for equality in the United States. A group was assembled under Claude Barnett, president of Associated Negro Press. Not surprisingly, it did not draw Roosevelt's parallel between African natives and black Americans, and viewed Africa much as any other Westerners would. Their V.I.P. treatment, after the routine daily harassments of black life in America at the time, must also have influenced their judgment. To Roosevelt's consternation, Villard recalled later, they were by and large impressed by colonial development and highly critical of U.S. neglect of Liberia.

In Ethiopia, reports from Consul Talbot Smith in Asmara showed that Haile Selassie was effectively re-establishing his authority – and faster than had been expected. The Emperor was pressing for the reopening of the Legation in the capital; he applied for Ethiopia to adhere to the Atlantic Charter and the embryonic United Nations. Britain was dragging its feet in Ethiopia: its Army wanted a British protectorate in the country; this cautioned the U.S. attitude. But Roosevelt's foreign policy was now becoming very liberal.

In September, Haile Selassie wrote a personal letter to Consul Smith. Earlier, the Emperor and Roosevelt had exchanged further messages, with the Emperor expressing thanks that the United States had never recognized the Italian occupation of his kingdom. By October, Roosevelt had 'accepted' Ethiopian membership of the United Nations.

Several more communications passed between Roosevelt and the Ethiopian leader, who had emerged as one of the Second World War hero-figures. The U.S. supplied increased aid, and technical advisors. Smith recommended that 'We should use Ethiopia as an example of what the United Nations are to do for natives that have been overrun by the Axis juggernaut'. The Legation was reopened, with John K. Caldwell as Minister Resident.

. . . . .

One major policymaker now beginning to figure in African affairs as well as other facets of U.S. political life was W. Averell Harriman, a tall, self-confident Rooseveltian Brahmin with a substantial fortune in railroad money and sharp natural intelligence. As far back as the spring of 1941, Harriman had been to Africa at the request of Churchill – loaned to Britain by Roosevelt – for a survey of what could be done to satisfy British army needs. Traveling in a PB-Y, Harriman had visited Bathurst (Gambia), Freetown (Sierra Leone), Takoradi (Gold Coast), Lagos and Kano (Nigeria) and Khartum (Sudan). Then he had flown down the Nile to Cairo and back up Eritrea with Britain's General Wavell. He successfully recommended that the U.S. Navy take over Ethiopia's port, Massawa, to prevent the German army in Egypt using it as an escape channel. Thanks partly to this visit, the U.S. built an airport at nearby Asmara.

A keen, determined judge of character, Harriman was immensely impressed by Haile Selassie, a factor which helped influence Roosevelt's later attitude to the Emperor. Harriman was at once caught up in the mystique and idealism of the man who had fought Mussolini and made a tragic appeal to the League of Nations. Recalling this trip, Harriman noted of Haile Selassie much later: 'He's really the most durable statesman of our time. What's interesting is that Africans admire him as much as we do – for his durability and above all for his nationalism.' Partly because of Harriman's influence, Ethiopia was to become, in the Fifties and Sixties, the lynchpin of U.S. policy in the Red Sea zone.

Traveling with Roosevelt, Harriman met Sultan Mohammed V of Morocco and the infant Crown Prince – later, Hassan II. Mohammed, of course, stressed the need for Moroccan independence. Harriman was to recount later that Roosevelt had 'great insight into the postwar world. He saw the need for the end of European colonization'. Churchill, notoriously short-sighted on this point, had angrily disputed Roosevelt's opinion. Harriman remembered Roosevelt as especially anxious to prevent the return of France to Indochina; but the British favored this, and President Truman – who 'never did know much about Asia' – subsequently gave way, Harriman recalled. Fortunately, Truman's acceptance of Churchill's infallibility, and his consequent repudiation of President Roosevelt's prescience, was to have a less cataclysmic effect in Africa than it later did in Southeast Asia.

The End of the War in North Africa

Up in Morocco, relations with Spain continued to be fractious; but they improved with the Sultan himself, who sent the Berber Pasha of Marrakesh, *haj* Thami Al Glawi, to the Legation with an important request. The Sultan wanted Morocco to be placed under the joint protection of the United States, Great Britain, France and Spain – since France alone, the Sultan noted, was no longer able to give any meaningful protection, and the country was 'unprepared for total independence' under the present war conditions. Both the U.S. and Britain were afraid of offending France. (Though Al Glawi, the Sultan reported that the French were much less afraid of offending the United States, against whom, he said, they had tried to influence the ruler. It was an augury of many postwar Franco-American clashes in Africa.)

The Sultan's immediate need was for a 'high-ranking' U.S. diplomat in Rabat with whom he could have direct contact. On June 24, 1943, during ceremonies at Oujda which Murphy attended, the Sultan made overtures to Roosevelt's representative and asked him for private talks. Moving a step onward from his earlier proposal, he let it be known that he would welcome the old French protectorate being replaced by a postwar American administration.

In October, Second Secretary C. Burke Eldrick of the Tangier Legation had a long talk with the Glawi, who again pressed for the United States to replace the repressive French and the impoverished Spanish and unify the kingdom under a single protectorate. The Glawi explained that he was being used as a go-between because the French would not allow the Sultan to speak to Americans except in the presence of French officials. The Sultan felt that eventually Morocco could qualify for full independence. *Chargé* Rives Childs in Tangier was authorized to continue these discussions.

In 1944, with the liberation of France in sight, lend–lease was extended to all French overseas territories. A special economic mission was sent to Tunisia, Algeria and Morocco.

In May that year, Childs, now counselor of Legation, took up a major complaint with the Spanish authorities. Spanish Morocco's anti-aircaft batteries – including some in what was legally, still, the International Zone – had been firing on Allied aircraft. These had come into range while in hot pursuit of German submarines seeking refuge inside Spanish Moroccan waters. But the Spanish remained truculent and only agreed to refrain from firing at aircraft above the water: they would still fire at any that crossed the Moroccan coast. In retrospect, the extraordinary negotiation is chiefly interesting for the way it reflects the curious ambiguities of the time: Spanish acts of war against Allied aircraft could presumably have been stopped by a simple ultimatum. The caution reflects much of the spirit with which Washington still approached even discredited powers in Africa – in this case, correctly fearing that the Franco regime would outlast all contemporary predictions.

Spain was not the only Axis sympathizer in the African area with which the U.S. was to have trouble. Long and exasperating negotiations were to be carried on with Portugal for the use of air bases on Terceira and Santa Maria, in the Azores, to patrol the African Atlantic for submarines.

Relations were much better with Ethiopia. In August, 1944, Haile Selassie gave the United States the grounds and buildings of the Legation, in perpetuity, along with gifts of furniture and silverware. He and Roosevelt exchanged 'great and good friend' letters. That year, Liberia also adhered to the U.N. and the Charter.

In Morocco, meanwhile, nationalist pressure was renewed on Consul-General H. Earle Russell in Casablanca. The Sultan wanted greater participation for Moroccans in their own affairs and still favored an international protectorate (rather than French or Spanish administrations) if a simple U.S. protectorate was out of the question. Later, Ahmed Balafrej and Mohammed Lyazidi informed Consul Mayer in Rabat that they intended publishing an international plea for revision of Morocco's status. At this point, it was genuinely unclear how far the Sultan was prepared to go in supporting them, and there was a pretext for U.S. caution. The two nationalists were anxious to counter, in advance, anticipated French propaganda that they had been 'put up to it' by German agents.

Both the British and American Legations informed the French of the development, without naming names, and urged there should be no repression, arguing that it was not in the French interest to make martyrs of the nationalists. Consul Mayer was clearly unsympathetic to Muslim nationalist hopes. There was probably a genuine fear, in most of his generation of diplomats, of the aspirations unleashed all over the world by the global conflict, by Britain's partial defeat in the Orient and by France's military annihilation in 1940.

The despatches from Russell and Childs reflect this grim historic ambivalence – and their reports say that the British diplomats felt the same about Morocco. Individual U.S. army and air force officers, however, encouraged Moroccan nationalism, sharing the revulsion of Moroccan intellectuals at the preservation in power of many Vichyite officials. There were demonstrations in Rabat. As only a decade of power remained for the French in any case, and as France was to depart from Morocco under a cloud of suspicion – leaving the United States (as in Indochina) to pick up some of the shattered pieces – hindsight indicates that foresight was missing. Some sort of an opportunity was surely missed. One result, useful to the West, of satisfying the Sultan's wishes might have been the continued internationalization of Tangier after the kingdom's independence – which finally came to pass in 1956.

In February, 1945, on his way back from Yalta, Roosevelt held talks at Ismailia with King Farouk of Egypt, King Abdul Aziz al Saud of Saudi Arabia and Emperor Haile Selassie. Haile Selassie's main request was for a port in Eritrea; in answer to Roosevelt's question, he said a railroad to such a port would be feasible. It was now broadly accepted by the Allies that Ethiopia was to have Eritrea as war reparations. Haile Selassie wanted Somalia as well.

Farouk wanted the U.S. Legation in Cairo raised to Embassy level. The British, under whose virtual protectorate he held the throne, indicated that they approved. But the French opposed the upgrading of the U.S. Legations in Syria and Lebanon, wanting only the French missions to have Embassy status. U.S. Legations in Europe had by then virtually all been raised to the level of Embassies, and the development was under active discussion for the rest of the world.

The director of the Office of Near Eastern and African Affairs, Loy W. Henderson, discreetly encouraged Arab self-government moves. The French repressed immediate postwar nationalist movements in Algeria harshly, with methods that reminded U.S. diplomats of the Nazis: the U.S. Department of State, under James Byrnes, leaned on Paris – without much success – to be more realistic. Byrnes actively pursued such policies with personal travel, flying often to key capitals. His staff quipped that 'State fiddles while Byrnes roams'.

A Carolinian with pronounced segregationist beliefs, the new Secretary of State was to prove less sympathetic to Liberia than to the Arabs. In April, 1945, he wrote a scathing memorandum for Roosevelt detailing the 'unfavorable' social, political and economic conditions in the black republic, scoring the 'inefficiency and lack of initiative of the ruling group, the corruption in government circles, the scandalous treatment of the native inhabitants and the lack of democratic practices'. Liberia, he noted, was widely seen as a U.S. responsibility. *Chargé* Felix Cole had just concluded his assignment there with a highly critical report, and presumably drafted all or most of Byrnes' memo.

In May, Henry Villard, now chief of the new Division of African Affairs, went to San Francisco, where the U.N. was in gestation, to lobby Liberian Vice-President Charles L. Simpson. He urged him against accepting a British colonial advisor, as the new President, 'Shad' Tubman, was reportedly about to do. Simpson said he agreed with Villard. No such appointment was subsequently made.

The Tubman era opened up shirtleeved diplomacy and put a high value on common sense. In Monrovia, the President frequently drove up to the U.S. Legation, on a bluff overlooking the Atlantic, and initiated talks himself. Even in conservative Liberia, a wind of change was now apparent.

At the peace conference, the U.S. delegation, on Henderson's advice, backed Ethiopia's claim to Eritrea, about which Haile Selassie had written fervently to Truman. Italy, which had switched sides in the conflict toward the end, kept Somalia, which was scheduled for independence in 1960. Libya was given to Britain as a trusteeship territory for six years. The old League mandates in Africa became U.N. ones; but in former 'German Southwest', South Africa transformed its League mandate into an annexation. The U.S., like the U.K. and France, acquiesced.

Moves began to restore internationality to Tangier and to revise the old statute of 1923, which gave over-representation to Spain and France. Russia now had to be brought in to join the Zone's ruling powers. France opposed a plan to bring in U.N. involvement, fearing that it would lead to U.N. jurisdiction for all Morocco (a prospect which the Sultan had already told United States diplomats that he would welcome). A conference was held in Paris in August, 1945, at which the Russians opposed a continued Spanish presence in Tangier because of Franco's war record (he had sent volunteers to fight on Germany's Russian front). A compromise was reached, with U.S. assistance. At the end of the year, the Spanish Moroccan troops in the Zone were replaced by French *goumiers*.

In 1946 came renewed and difficult tractations with Portugal over Santa Maria and the Lagens airfield on Terceira, now bases in the gathering conflict with Moscow. In October, the Department of State brought a First Secretary of the British Embassy, Donald Maclean – then a Soviet master spy – in on the Azores discussions, and U.S. officials agreed to keep Maclean informed of developments. The era of the cold war was now very much at hand, and was to affect U.S. policy in Africa, as elsewhere.

II

Every African leader guided by a conscience must recognize now the value of cooperation with the United States and see that American assistance is, contrary to what we are told, the most disinterested, the most effective and the most responsive to our real needs.

Ahmed Sekou Touré

PART FOUR
1946–1963
America and African Nationalism

Looking back, looking forward

To sum up, for the first century of its existence, the United States saw Africa as Europe did – and as Africa saw Europe and America. It was first and foremost a mercantile relationship. Africa was a prime source of certain major and minor imports – gum, slaves, ivory, palm – and a useful and growing (if predominantly barter) market for textiles and other finished goods. U.S. policy in Africa was directed toward preserving trade against European competition or proto-colonial protectionism. Even more than the African trade of Europe, the African trade of the United States was the preserve of a small number of cities.

The American role in both West and East Africa, in the precolonial period, had been as considerable as that of France and almost as influential as that of Britain: America had outdistanced, in its role in nineteenth-century Africa, the roles of Portugal, Germany, Belgium, Italy and Spain, or the roles of the minor Euro-African powers like Denmark and Brandenburg. But Africa had played less of a role in American commerce than it had in the trade of Europe, especially as Abolition had become effective. The only special United States stake in Africa had been Liberia, which American interests had founded and the federal Government had protected, albeit in a distant manner.

After Berlin, colonial protectionism had limited American markets in Africa. Politics had dictated that Africa should now be realistically regarded as an annex of Europe. Of the great western-hemisphere powers, the U.S. had remained the only anti-colonial nation, and this puissant tradition had showed up at many key stages: indeed, it helps explain America's reluctance to do, in Liberia, as much as the Liberians themselves requested. But the First World War had brought America politically closer to Britain and France; and the second world war had forced a conflict between official American awareness that its own anti-imperial precedent was about to triumph in Africa, and the immediate, opportunistic need to temper realism with a judicious element of injustice – to prop up economically devastated western Europe, especially France.

Parts of Africa had enjoyed a strategic significance in the early decades of America's existence, when the Mediterranean was the main Atlantic gateway to war-torn Europe – with the old, intimate enemy Britain blockading half of the continent. This had thrust America into conflict with the corsairs of the Barbary Shore. There were to be other occasions that challenged the New World's isolationist ideals, but none seriously.

For a significant period in the nineteenth century, America had been the main foreign power in Zanzibar; but traditionally, its closest African links have been with Atlantic Africa. The Barbary relationship had soon shriveled to a continuing strategic concern with Morocco and – for a few decades at the end of the century – a useful and influential role at the khedivial court of Cairo.

Colonization schemes, beginning with Paul Cuffee, and missionary enterprises had reflected the English-speaking world's preoccupation with humanitarian ideals – an ethical counterpoise to trade which has no equivalent of any importance in the African episodes of the European continental powers. Despite Africa's remoteness, Americans had also figured largely among those who opened up the continent's interior; and the bestknown explorer in the world, Henry Morton Stanley, was an American by adoption and naturalization. The role of the explorers had been crucial, for the sub-Sahara continent produced no great travelers or navigators of its own. To the frontiersman spirit of America, Africa had been an obvious lure.

Basically, the links between the United States and Africa had been those of a maritime power to a region without a maritime tradition. To re-use a phrase, Africa had, historically, behaved as a female continent – the passive recipient of ships, travelers, explorers, missionaries and above all men of trade, who handled both Africa's imports and exports. The great indigenous industries of Africa had been gold-mining and slaving; when the market for slaves had died in the western hemisphere, and the need for Africa's more industrial primary resources had replaced the need for men, Africa had historically found itself ripe for conquest. The anti-imperialistic United States had taken no part in this except for the Arthur–Kasson–Sanford–Stanley initiatives at Berlin, which had soon been rejected by the Congress. Thus, Africa's brief but historically ultra-significant colonial period from the 1890s to the 1960s saw a substantial drop in America's influence and interest in Africa.

The closest American links in the modern era are with Ethiopia, Morocco, Tunisia, the Congo (now Zaire), Nigeria, Liberia and Kenya. In three of these seven cases – Ethiopia, Morocco and Liberia – these were the enduring links of pre-nationalist times. In Ethiopia's case the links came late, and fitfully, but both Menelik and Haile Selassie were clearly aware of the special advantage of an American over a European link. So too were the mid-twentieth century rulers of Morocco. The link with Liberia was always as strong as a persistent Liberia could induce a reluctant America to let it be.

Above all, what stands out, in contrast to the diplomacy of Europe in Africa from the late eighteenth century to World War Two, was the official timidity of the United States, even when it became incontestably the world's leading power. It was not that America's interests in Africa were, ever, all that much less than Europe's (it was only the strictly non-colonial approach that diminished America's leverage), or that the U.S. could be substantially less involved in a continent that fulfilled an obvious economic role for all the developed world: but an element of amateurish hesitation had overhung those little consulates, making the prestigious Stars and Stripes on the flagpoles oddly incongruous.

There had been, in sum, inadequate reactions to local

challenges, inadequate self-confidence or humor in dealing with local vicissitudes, and almost always inadequate finance: America's foreign policy, even in Europe, had been an under-capitalized concern. America's farflung Consuls had reported Morocco's declaration of war on the United States, the continual contest for markets and alliances, an African prince's offer of marriage to Alice Roosevelt, or – more frequently – the need for funds to keep body and soul together: and they had done all this as though guilty of involving America in the world. The old State Department set this pattern: its ministers and consuls were the envoys, not of the steel mills of Pittsburgh or the Oklahoma oilfields or of Wall Street, but of Arcadia.

As the burgeoning mid-twentieth century brought its new challenges, the need for a new and more professional breed of Brahmins was apparent – one that would put the poised and confident journeymen of Europe 'back' where they belonged. And by and large this breed was, in fact, to emerge quickly – along with a budget that would have made poor Peter Strickland gasp. For the first time, the State Department began to forge a policy for Africa.

The United States, innately anticolonialist by education, was a generation ahead of the Frenchmen, Britons and Belgians who emerged from the second world war – the British sorely humiliated in the East, the French and the Belgians salvaged after conquest itself only by American liberation forces. America's acceptance of the inevitable implications of World War Two was well demonstrated by the end of the U.S. protectorate over the Philippines. In regard to Africa, America's instinctive acceptance of decolonization brought enmity from the governments of the colonial powers and their often extremely right-wing citizens in Africa itself. The old myth of America seeking its own imperial domains was raised again. Because of the current importance of the Communist threat, the U.S. officially modified its anticolonial stance to accommodate the decolonizing hesitancies of its allies. This of course played into the hands of Russian – and later Chinese – propaganda.

When the U.S.–Soviet confrontation finally came in the Congo, however, President Eisenhower, and later President Kennedy, were able to move more and more decisively – and in the direction desired by most of Africa. Yet the Congolese situation was embarrassing also, because of the humiliation heaped on a N.A.T.O. ally, Belgium. The event illustrated superlatively well the interdepartmental clashes between European and African 'desks' at State, and between civil and military views as to what the crisis was all about; in the Sixties, these clashes were to characterize much of the policymaking in African affairs.

Decisions on the future of colonial rule had had to be taken, to some degree, during the war. Roosevelt had preserved his anticolonial instincts, in spite of Cordell Hull's cool indifference to what is now called the Third World, and Jimmy Byrnes' contempt for black Africa – the fruit of a white-Southern upbringing. F. D. R. had seen the Atlantic Charter as West Africa's leading nationalist of the day, Nnamdi Azikiwe, saw it – a clear manifesto against imperialism. He had seen, too, the role that America's attitudes about race – often frightful, but essentially more easygoing than those of Europe in Africa – could have in the tense African colonies of France, Britain, Belgium and Portugal.

Robert Murphy was obliged, for pragmatic reasons of war, to buck the historic trend and help restore French rule in North Africa. At the time, both Roosevelt and his circle of advisors were also influenced by Churchill, who had badly misjudged the turn of history which the war had brought. During the Marshall Plan years, the United States accepted that exploitation of colonial territories had a role to play in the economic recovery of European allies, especially France. Thus the primacy of defeating Hitler, and later Stalin's own imperial policy, delayed African independence by inhibiting the American commitment to it: but few, at the time, in the African division of the State Department, expected that the move from total dependence to nationhood would happen so fast. Like most African politicians, most Washington observers would have been satisfied with a gradual development of internal self-government, with ultimate independence being made consonant on economic viability. When the trend gathered speed, Washington gathered fresh pretexts for caution.

African development in the Truman years was largely paid for, directly or indirectly, by the United States – especially development in North Africa. But not all this aid was a blessing to the citizens. Since Algeria was constitutionally part of metropolitan

France, French troops assigned to N.A.T.O. could be stationed there, performing a repressive colonial role in the guise of national self-defense – deployed across the 'province' (*département*) with the latest American weaponry. Similarly, U.S. military aid led to Washington unintentionally funding France's purely colonial war against the Viet Minh: constantly urging Paris to negotiate had little effect while N.A.T.O. obligations involved the United States in furnishing 'defensive' arms that could be used to defend 'France' in Cochin-China.

In other ways, however, the U.S. emerged as the only western power actively working for decolonization. Over British and French objections, Washington pushed through a United Nations measure obliging trusteeship powers to make annual reports on the U.N. territories they governed, and to accept U.N. supervision to ensure that the territories were being prepared for independence. This measure was aimed predominantly at France and Belgium, both anxious to set the clock back in Africa and elsewhere. The measure played a crucial political role in Kamerun and especially Togo, whose promise of independence led to a 1958 referendum which brought independence to all of French Africa two years later.

A constant but unexpressed French fear was that Washington failed to appreciate the depths of the French dilemma 'overseas'. Since Britain had been largely victorious in the war, and had only been defeated (colonially) in the Orient, London had no humiliation to avenge by a power play in the tropical world. France still sought to assert itself as a 'power' in the Nineteen Thirties sense. Britain's experience contained famous and massive precedents for decolonization, and World War Two had ended with the virtual promise of nationhood for India – in comparison with which the world's other colonies seemed fairly inconsequential.

Washington, in the late Forties and the Fifties, tended to let its Africa policy follow that of Britain, partly because of the strong World War Two and linguistic tie, but partly also because of the British air of self-confidence about the decolonization trend. To some extent, as noted, Britain's self-confidence was genuine: when Nigeria became independent and decided it would have an air force, few eyebrows were raised in London when an ex-Luftwaffe ace was hired by Lagos to train its pilots. No one who is cognizant with the official attitudes of

France in Africa would have much difficulty imagining what Paris reaction would have been if a formerly French territory had chosen a non-Frenchman for such a task – even if the nominee had come from one of the Allied forces.

But even the British acceptance of decolonization was gradualistic, and hedged about with reservations regarding the settler territories, especially Kenya. There were many ways in which London hesitated – and when it did, Washington tended to hesitate as well. (The British could even be oddly French, on occasion: as late as the mid-Sixties, Zambia's High Commissioner-designate to London, Ali Simbule, got himself into the history books by calling Britain's supine stance on Rhodesia that of a 'toothless bulldog': the phrase had such an obvious ring of gentle truth that British conservatives covered themselves in ridicule by forcing Simbule's reappointment elsewhere. Americans could be similarly vulnerable. When former State Secretary Dean Acheson, in retirement, remarked that Britain had lost an empire and failed to find a role, this also was so apt a comment that it had official Britain protesting – implying a secret regret at the loss of Empire. More recently, official Britons have complained vehemently against Senator Edward Kennedy appropriately calling Northern Ireland 'Britains' Viet Nam'.)

What French and Belgian 'reactionary' attitudes and British ambivalence implied was that there was a leadership role that the U.S. could and should take in Africa. Unfortunately, few State Department officers knew anything of black Africa, with the marginal exception of Liberia. It was broadly assumed that British Africa wore a Cedric Hardwicke look of well-brushed efficiency and stuffiness, that French Africa was seedy and easygoing and Belgian Africa vaguely similar. In reality, the harshest or stuffiest parts of Africa were the settler zones, regardless of flag – France's Algeria, Belgium's Congo, Britain's Kenya and the Rhodesias. In the normal, 'trade' colonies. French and Belgian rule was harsher than that of the British, administration tighter and more military. Racial segregation was more rigid in Dahomey than in Nigeria, in Ivory Coast or Senegal than in the Gold Coast. French administrators worked hard to find out such obscure police-state details as how many bicycles and sewing machines each of their colonial citizens possessed – an effort which cost French taxpayers more than the few extra dollars which two-bicycle farmers were obliged to pay in local taxes. The British used a skeletal administration and as much indirect rule as possible: outside the settler zones, Britain had much more relaxed, easygoing colonies than France or Belgium. Attitudes to natives were also influenced by the nature of the character of the colonial: overseas service was seen as a disgrace in France, and colonial careers largely attracted rednecks, who were less sympathetic to Africa than the French at home. Britain had built a mystique around outposts of empire: virtually, only the products of the country's private schools were accepted for most colonial jobs. U.S. observers were often confused by the resultant, variegated image: the notion that scions of ancient families should be less prejudiced than self-made or un-made men was nothing new – the American civil liberties struggle was largely funded by inherited wealth. But although Britain's behavior in Africa did not entirely contradict its old, repugnant, colonial image for Americans, France's behavior clashed with the American illusion of the humane French democrat. All in all, the most self-critically objective American observers of the time could hardly fail to reach the conclusion that an American political system, whatever its faults, might have suited Africa better than the curiously outdated systems imposed in African colonies by Britain, Belgium, Italy, Portugal and France. One of Europe's fears was that Africa might come to notice this as well: some African constitutional lawyers ultimately did.

Policy speeches in the early Eisenhower years – by Assistant Secretary Henry A. Byroade and his successor George V. Allen in particular – stressed the American quandary: the logic of anticolonialism, on which the U.S. was born, was constantly counterbalanced by the Cold War commitment to colonial powers, including a semi-alliance with Spain. Yet it was under Eisenhower that a more pragmatic policy toward Africa began to emerge: Washington added its pressure to the trend toward independence in Tunisia and Morocco. President Eisenhower was especially instrumental in persuading the French to restore Sultan Mohammed V, in place of the 'puppet' Moulay ben Arafa. Both Maghribi countries recovered nationhood in 1956, along with the Anglo-Egyptian condominium of the Sudan. Also in 1956, the United States joined the Soviet Union in voting against France for its abuse of its Togo mandate.

Congressional interests in Africa also began to develop in this period, notably through the efforts of Senator Theodore Green of Rhode Island. This enabled President Eisenhower to increase aid to Africa. From 1953 to 1957, direct loans and grants to Africa (mostly administered by colonial powers) had totaled $120,300,000. They rose to approximately $100m. for fiscal 1958 alone, rising further the following year to $185m. and to $211m. in 1960. In 1961, because of the Congo crisis, additional appropriations alone came to nearly $200m. The U.S. was to play a major and constructive role in the tragic Congolese events, in contrast to the largely mischievous pro-Katanga activities of Britain and France.

Independence in Libya and Ghana: the Holmes Report

Tunisia, Morocco and Sudan had not been the first African independence achievements of the post-war age. Aside from Egypt's revolution of 1952, overthrowing King Farouk and British overlordship, Libya had recovered sovereignty in 1951. The U.S. had played an important role in assuring Libya's independence.

Liberated from Italian colonization by British forces in 1943, Libya had a 'straight' military occupation afterward, not a colonial mandate. British forces occupied Cyrenaica and Tripolitania, French forces the upcountry Fezzan.

Other proposals had clashed. Britain had wanted to acquire the two provinces it occupied and France coveted the Fezzan. The United States proposed a ten-year U.N. trusteeship, then independence. If there was to be a U.N. mandate, France, Britain and Italy all wanted it. Moscow proposed a 'troika' trusteeship – the Soviet Union in Tripolitania, Britain in Cyrenaica, France in the Fezzan. France and Britain were then prepared to accept a 'troika' decade – if the U.S. replaced the Soviet Union in Tripolitania. This was unacceptable to Congress.

The occupation, conducted in the presence of a noted U.N.

Commissioner, Adrian Pelt of the Netherlands, ended on schedule after six years. Libya was voted a member of the United Nations by fortyeight votes to one. The opposition came from France, then beginning a decade of obstructionism to independence in Africa (in this case, because of the propinquity of nationalist Tunisia.)

The first U.S. Minister (1952–55) to King Idris was the State Department's Africa veteran Harry Villard. Still a maverick, Villard was in Tripoli in September, 1953, when the King's first premier, Mahmud Muntasir, threatened to resign in a disagreement over royal powers, and made plans to take off for Rome – whence he actually sent back his resignation. Villard wired the Department for permission to go after him and talk him into coming back. No reply arrived in time. Villard went anyway, and his mission was successful: Muntasir returned with Villard and resumed his post – but finally quit the following year. Villard, meanwhile, had returned from Rome to find a Department cable saying that 'under no circumstances' should he leave his post.

While in Libya, Villard also negotiated the lease, for the U.S. Air Force, of Wheelus Base – with an assist from a visiting Vice-President Richard Nixon. The Wheelus agreement was signed in Benghazi on September 9, 1954.

This was not to be the end of Villard's African career. At the War College as civilian Deputy Commandant until 1958 he was, he recalls, offered the new post of Assistant Secretary of State for African Affairs, which he at once accepted. On his return from leading a War College tour of Asia, however, he found he had been shelved in favor of Julius Holmes, author of a perspicaceous report on current developments in Africa. But the Senate opposed Holmes, and Joseph Satterthwaite finally got the job. Villard went to Geneva as Consul-General and as U.S. Representative to the United Nations office there. From 1960 to 1961, he was America's first Ambassador in Dakar, Senegal.

In early 1957, Vice-President Nixon toured Morocco, Ghana, Liberia, Uganda, Ethiopia, Sudan, Libya and Tunisia. In Ghana, he attended independence ceremonies on March 6. Nixon expressed enthusiasm about the African leaders he met. His report for President Eisenhower foresaw a need for the

U.S. to help independent Africa, especially those countries whose 'backlash' relations with the former metropoles might perhaps be acrimonious – Morocco, Tunisia, eventually French black Africa and British East Africa. He shrewdly foresaw the importance of the coming battle for the 'soul' of Africa's labor movements: this is, of course, an area in which the United States is considerably more progressive than the world's Communist regimes; but although this progressiveness was to prove an attraction to rank and file unionists and labor leaders, it was often less alluring to governments – which tended to prefer the controlled labor movements of 'socialist' economies.

The newly created Bureau of African Affairs was already beginning to feel the strain of competing with the older divisions at State, especially 'Europe'. Senator John F. Kennedy's July 2, 1957 statement supporting independence for Algeria had split the Department, if not exactly down the middle, at least somewhere on the side. There was also a counterpoise within the Division itself. In December, 1957, Deputy Assistant Secretary of State Joseph Palmer II had issued a public warning against 'premature independence' in the tropical world, and had urged in particular that the United States should try to avoid involvement in the growing racial crisis in South Africa. In the Sixties, Palmer was to become Assistant Secretary, in charge of the Africa Bureau, where he put the brakes on the impetus given to policy by Kennedy. His successor as Deputy Assistant, Julius C. Holmes, showed himself more sympathetic to African aspirations.

During 1957, as a Special Assistant, Holmes had traveled at length in the continent and had written a report for Secretary Foster Dulles, correctly predicting that African independence was closer at hand than Britain and France seemed to think. He recommended leaning on London and Paris not to resist the dictates of history. Britain's acceptance of independence for the Sudan the year before, and for Ghana that year, helped make Holmes' suggestions acceptable: but in 1958, Schlesinger's memoirs of Kennedy reveal, de Gaulle threatened to leave N.A.T.O. if Washington recognized independent Guinea: this led to unfortunate delays in recognition. By 1960, de Gaulle had capitulated in Africa, except in Algeria, and the U.S. position became easier.

Holmes recommended substantial area training for diplomats, especially those in the middle grades, and said young officers should be recruited who were prepared to devote a substantial part of their careers to African area specialization. The dearth of African specialists was then obvious. Of the 2,600 officers submitting post preference forms in 1958, Professor McKay has noted, only 146 indicated Africa *among* their choices. By 1962, there were 286 F.S.O's in Africa – 7·8 per cent of all officers and 11·8 per cent of all officers abroad. By then, roughly ten per cent were indicating post interest in Africa.

At this point, there were 3,099 F.S.O's in all: only 537 had African experience; only thirty-two had over five years' duty in the continent; only one had over ten years' experience of African affairs – Harry Villard.

The Holmes Report – declassified for the purpose of this study – pragmatically divided Africa four ways – Arabo-Berber and black, English and French-speaking; there was a separate section comprising the independent nations of Ethiopia and Liberia, and finally the settler zone.

Holmes wrote prophetically that 'I am convinced that in the long term all of the colonial and trust territories in Africa will achieve either complete independence or independence qualified only by voluntary but equal association with the metropolitan powers'. He thought Belgium would hold out against independence longer than France and Britain, and Portugal longest of all.

Equally prophetically and pertinently, Holmes reported that 'this movement toward self-government is being carried forward within the framework of Western European political systems and the social and economic advances are based on concepts which Europeans have developed over the centuries and which are suited to them and expressive of them. There is grave doubt that these systems and concepts will turn out to be valid for Africa. It may be that eventually there will evolve political, social and economic systems consistent with and expressive of the African personality which still preserve the essentials of democracy and individual liberty. But before such a happy result can be achieved, I foresee a very difficult and probably long period of uncertainty, bad management, retrogression and conflict with a strong chance of violence in some areas. There will be plenty of troubled waters for Communist fishing. In my opinion the most difficult problem in the modernization of Africa, and the greatest factor making for instability, is de-tribalization.'

Holmes noted the problems inherent in abandoning abruptly 'ancient folkways which provided a sense of social, economic and religious security'. He found most nationalist leaders to be moderates who deserved sympathetic encouragement from the colonial powers and the U.S. – and aid, in order for them to satisfy the economic and social demands of their populations.

The 'enabling law' (*loi-cadre*) had been passed by France the year before, introducing a degree of self-government in the French territories. The sharply observant diplomat recorded that 'the *loi-cadre* had been considered in Paris to . . . [have established] the relationships between France and its African possessions for the indefinite future. In Africa, it is viewed as only a step toward complete self-government.' Holmes added that 'the serious problem in the political evolution of the French African territories is that neither the French nor the Africans can foresee the shape of their eventual relationship with the metropole . . . The status of British territories after independence is clear: membership in the Commonwealth. Even though no one has been able to define Commonwealth membership, it is an accepted goal . . . The French West Africans would like to see the French Union changed into a Confederation in which the Republic would be one unit . . . There is a good deal of dynamism behind this idea and we may see some interesting developments when it encounters in-grained French centralism and basic conservatism . . . Either the French Union will be changed to permit substantially the same degree of autonomy for its African territories as that enjoyed by members of the Commonwealth, or those territories will break away entirely and become separate independent states. In either contingency, there is a strong likelihood of fragmentation of the eight territories of French West Africa and the four of French Equatorial Africa.'

Holmes foresaw the problems posed by white settlers in Capricorn Africa, but not the problems caused by Asian settlement. He predicted that nationalism in the Congo would eventually expand to become something which the imprudent Belgians would be unable to contain. He added: 'The Belgians will be slow to move, but I believe they will move in an effort to preserve their economic position and political influence. They will be stubborn, but Belgians have a way of looking out for their equities.'

Of the Portuguese, he said that they 'will probably be the last to give in to African self-rule but sooner or later they will have to do so'.

On South Africa, he correctly foresaw that 'the Nationalist Party will remain in power probably with an increase in seats resulting from gerrymandering'. Holmes noted that *apartheid* was a 'dead-end policy' involving 'lip-service' to separation, which the need for black labor made impossible.

He added: 'In spite of harassment by the Government, there is growing confidence of the African, Asian and "Colored" leaders.' The trend toward independence throughout the continent encouraged this. The situation in South Africa was encouraging Communism and 'a burning hatred for the whites'. Holmes observed that 'the atmosphere of solemn hostility was very apparent in Johannesburg'. A violent explosion was inevitable.

Holmes also saw the appeal of Islam for black Africa: 'the brotherhood of Islam is real'; it absorbed African customs and religion and permitted polygamy; conversion gave prestige; it wasn't white. Islam was unlikely to prove a stepping stone for Egyptian influence, he wrote presciently (he must have been almost alone in thinking that at the time); but a black Mahdi might arise. If Soviet plans for Africa were to be thwarted, the Western powers should act in concurrence: 'This will require an understanding [on the part of the colonial powers] of our objectives, and a higher degree of confidence in our motives in Africa than now exists.'

On tribalism at a higher level, Holmes wrote that 'the black African's attitude toward the white man shades from universal envy through mistrust and fear to burning hate. That is a sweeping statement, but I believe it to be true and of such importance that we should have it constantly in mind as background to our actions and decisions as the evolution of Africa proceeds.'

On North Africa, Holmes reported that 'I want to express the opinion that France cannot win with present attitudes and methods. Unless there is a change and some form of negotiated settlement (with Algeria) is reached, the French position in North Africa will be lost, with the grave danger that the area will be lost to the West as well.' Britain and the U.S. should lean on France 'to change its attitude; and should that attempt fail, [we should] serve notice that we propose to do what we can to save the North African littoral in the name of Western security.'

Holmes called for a high quality of U.S. personnel for Africa and urgent contingency planning to 'avoid the need to engage in expensive and inefficient rescue operations'.

Holmes had, as we can now see in retrospect, called all the shots with astonishing accuracy; he was clairvoyant on independent Africa's uneasy political evolution; he depicted the coming problems of Africa's settler zone; he foresaw the Belgian fiasco in the Congo; he distinguished the grave dangers inherent in French stubbornness and dictatorial attitudes, both in black and Arab Africa.

Holmes' reflections on French political philosophy were particularly important for U.S. policy. Today, France remains the only member-state in the nine-nation European Community which still displays bullying and arbitrary attitudes toward opposition politics, the Press, and public liberties: the French regime, in other words, is set in an authoritarian mold long abandoned by the other modernized nations of western Europe. This predisposes governments in Paris toward domineering policies in independent Africa, thus posing problems for the West; these characterial defects of the French body politic have resulted in cool Franco-American relations in Africa in recent years.

Holmes also saw beneath the surface the intense racism still ambivalently present in the black African psyche, a self-hate trauma with a finite love–hate result. (This was to manifest itself particularly strongly in post-civil war Nigeria, a key country in the U.S. Africa policy.) Holmes' appeal for contingency planning was to be heeded, to some extent, in the Kennedy years; since then, crises have more often been met by studied apathy than by 'expensive and inefficient rescue operations' – though these may come. Holmes' other findings also helped fashion the best of U.S. policy in Africa in the early Sixties. As the Holmes Report subsequently gathered dust, the State Department tended to score less successes.

1960: the Growth of African Affairs

In 1958, Joseph C. Satterthwaite became the first Assistant Secretary of State for African Affairs. As mentioned earlier, Julius Holmes, who was Herter's choice, had proved unacceptable to the Senate, and the outspoken Villard had been first selected, then passed over. Joe Satterthwaite had shown an early grasp of the African situation. Loy Henderson recollected in the early Seventies how, at a staff meeting fifteen years before, Satterthwaite had been asked how many new African nations could be expected. 'He answered: about thirtyfive. We nearly fell out of our chairs,' Henderson recalled.

Although it became clear at once that Satterthwaite had no intention of rocking the European boat on the great rivers of Africa, the Soviet Union created a Department of African Affairs in its foreign ministry the same week. Satterthwaite handled the sensitivities of the European 'desks' carefully. But he set about getting aid to Africa increased, and giving the prose of the American delegation at United Nations a distinctly more pro-African sound. By the following year, the cautious Satterthwaite was even calling for a 'new relationship with the dynamic twentieth century Africa, based on the principles of equality, justice and mutual understanding.'

The year 1960 brought the famous cascade of seventeen independences, the Congo crisis and Patrice Lumumba's appeal to President Eisenhower to intervene. (Eisenhower successfully recommended that Lumumba appeal to the United Nations.) Dr. Waldemar Nielsen says: 'The Eisenhower administration in its final year scrambled to break free of its earlier paralyzed and contradictory policy.' The year saw the abandonment of Foster Dulles' opposition to neutralism – an effort to head off a spread of the Cold War contest.

On September 22, Eisenhower addressed the General Assembly of the United Nations and presented a five-point program for Africa. It was the first American attempt to synthesize a program for the continent. Eisenhower stressed multilateral action through the United Nations – unaware of how acutely competitive for aid two-score new African countries were about to be, and how opposed therefore to multilateral schemes. Ike spoke in favor of political non-interference in the new nations' affairs.

In December, the lame-duck Eisenhower administration abstained on the U.N. vote against 'colonialism' in general, at the telephoned request of Britain's premier Harold Macmillan – who ironically was perhaps the greatest decolonizer of his day. But by then the U.S. had fairly clearly identified itself with decolonization as an all-over, ultimate, global objective. Early the next year, Kennedy's delegation took an uncompromising stand against Portuguese colonialism. That year, the continuing antics of the Congo in turmoil harmed the African image more than anything had managed to do before: some of the American public enthusiasm for Africa began to flag. The senseless and savage murder – following odious mutilations – of thirteen Italian airmen bringing U.N. food and other supplies to Kivu province, at the end of 1960, had synthesized the Congo horror for the world: many more spectacularly brutal chapters were to follow. This made a 'forward' African policy more difficult for any major nation, including America. In France, Cartierism (more 'development aid' at home, less in Africa) became popular. In Britain, the popular Press showed sympathy for the settler societies. The 'new Africa', it was realized in Washington, had not yet come: what the world was living with was the last chapter of the old.

Nevertheless, the U.S. began to separate its policy more clearly from the policies of its Western allies. Under the impulsion of Ambassador Edmund Gullion in Léopoldville, the U.S. spearheaded the African drive, through the U.N., to put down Katangese secession. Kennedy's steadfastness over the Congo, despite Congolese atrocities, was the high point of U.S. influence in Africa – just as de Gaulle's refusal to pay France's share of the cost of the U.N. operation seems, in retrospect, to have marked the beginning of the French decline in the continent. That America stood by Africa's aspirations at this time was partly due to the perspicacity of Kennedy and the presence of an exceptional envoy on the spot, but also very largely to the political skills and instinct of the new President's Assistant Secretary for African Affairs, Governor G. Mennen Williams. Another important factor in American prestige in Africa was the Peace Corps, established in March, 1961, early in the Kennedy mandate.

Despite cold war considerations in the Congo, America's broad concern for African affairs had no strategic urgency. It principally reflected the degree to which the world's richest, strongest nation was obliged to have an effective policy for every region of the globe. It came at a time when the Bureau of African Affairs, despite the Holmes Report, was still essentially embryonic.

This is perhaps the moment to recall the vicissitudes in growth of the Bureau itself.

At the outbreak of war in 1939, America had had four Legations in Africa – Addis Ababa, Monrovia, Cairo and Pretoria. There had also been three Consulates-General, eight Consulates and one consular agency. During World War Two, some temporary posts were created, notably in Brazzaville, de Gaulle's 'French soil' headquarters. In 1938, as noted earlier, the Division of European Affairs at State had transferred Africa to the Division of Near Eastern Affairs, which gave the Balkans (part of the old Ottoman Empire) to the European division in exchange. At this juncture only one man of executive rank – Villard – concentrated his entire attention on Africa. At the time of the 'exchange', the Near East Division already had Egypt, Ethiopia and Liberia (having taken over Ethiopia earlier from the Division of Far East Affairs).

In 1944, the Division of Near East Affairs had been renamed 'Office of Near Eastern and African Affairs' – a promotion in status: the 'Office' now included an African 'Division', dealing with the whole continent except for South Africa, Algeria and Madagascar (all three of which came under Europe) and Egypt and the Sudan (still both part of the Near East itself). In 1949, the Office had become the Bureau of Near Eastern, South Asian and African Affairs, and the African 'Division' had become an 'Office'. In 1955, 'Europe' had transferred South Africa and Madagascar to 'Africa'. Algeria, of course, had still been a part of metropolitan France, and therefore had remained in 'Europe'.

In 1950, Assistant Secretary George C. McGhee had complained that 'no comprehensive program of African area studies [exists] in any American university'. He had appealed for foundation support to remedy this. At that time, only two American universities had courses in African studies. By 1960, there were still only six. In the eight years from 1955 to 1962, only 27 Foreign Service Officers benefited from university-level African studies programs. From then on, these programs were better attended – but many F.S.O.'s presumably rightly guessed that the passion for Africa would pass and that they might later be 'punished', at more sensitive periods of their career, for having the wrong specialty.

The development of American representation in Africa started unevenly. Eisenhower, in 1953, had actually cut diplomatic representation in Africa from 207 American officers and 361 local employees to 129 Americans and 121 'locals'. The mounting workload had soon showed these economies to be unrealistic.

In 1956, two 'Offices' for African affairs had been set up at State – for North Africa and for sub-Sahara Africa – with thirtyfour officers under a Deputy Assistant Secretary of State. A full Bureau of African Affairs was created on July 1, 1958, headed by a new Assistant Secretaryship. It had taken a year to get the appropriations from the Congress. It was to cover all of Africa except Egypt and the Sudan (still part of the Near East) and Algeria – still part of France. The Sudan was added in 1961, Algeria at independence in 1962.

Governor Williams' nomination to the Assistant Secretary post in 1960 – President Kennedy's first major appointment – made the Bureau a virtual ministry for the next five years. In all, the ebullient, flamboyant Michigan politician made fourteen trips to Africa, many of them long, comprehensive diplomatic safaris. Williams was ably assisted by a dedicated Deputy Assistant Secretary, J. Wayne Fredericks. Bureau of African Affairs personnel increased from sixtyone in 1958 to 150 in 1962.

At the change of administrations (at the beginning of 1961), ambassadors followed tradition in resigning their posts, in most cases to be reappointed. Anticipating that Kennedy might want to appoint many people of his own – both career men and 'political' – to the new missions, Eisenhower left over many ambassadorial appointments in Africa, both at new embassies and in others where replacements were due. It was consequently a period of confusion and delays that were not always understood by African governments; the hiatus left room for some early influence jockeying between the new Africa Bureau, its anxious parents – the Near East and European Bureaus – and the Pentagon.

In October, 1960, shortly before the change of administrations, Under-Secretary Loy W. Henderson toured Africa to make an administrative report. He recommended four-year assignments to permit diplomats to learn the special requirements of African posts, divided by home leave in the middle: unfortunately, this perspicacious proposal was never acted on – old-timers in the Service complained that Africa was a hardship post area, and that longer-than-usual tours of duty would be unfair.

Henderson had brought with him a substantial team for a journey that took ten weeks. His nineteen experts included political officers from African Affairs, four Pentagon and service aides, U.S.I.S., A.I.D. and C.I.A. representatives, along with top-echelon officers from Personnel and Buildings. Henderson went to Switzerland to see President Tubman – then in a clinic there – and got a cool reception in Guinea and Ghana because of the lively controversy over U.S. support of the U.N. peacekeeping mission in the Congo. In the Congo itself, Ambassador Timberlake's car unavoidably toppled a cyclist while taking Henderson to the airport: in the ensuing melee, the Marine driver, Clyde St. Lawrence, and a Léopoldville political officer, Frank Carlucci, were badly slashed by an angry crowd. They were rescued by a Vice-Consul, Alison Palmer.

The Under-Secretary toured all the seventeen countries that became independent in 1960 except Mauritania, which did not reach nationhood until December: Villard reported from Dakar that 'the supersensitive French would object to an official U.S. visit there before independence'.

It was Henderson's post-by-post reports that fixed, among other things, the size of a minimal embassy in Africa: an ambassador, a deputy chief of mission–political officer, an economic and commercial officer, an administrative and consular officer, with one other officer arriving later to enable leaves to be taken; there would be three secretaries, and a fourth when first leaves were due. In some cases, small embassies might include one or two service *attachés*. Henderson has been criticized since for putting an embassy 'everywhere' and for over-staffing. But this was the Cold War period, involving direct confrontation with the Russians and the Chinese, notably in the Congo. Recent attempts to have an Embassy Office in Bathurst (now Banjul) with only a *chargé d'affaires* and two Gambian typists led to two successive officers in charge having partial nervous breakdowns. Ambassadors accredited to more than one country are acceptable from countries of the size of Ghana or Ireland – but not, as Henderson sensed, from the United States.

The Kennedy Years: an Overview

President Kennedy's own interest in Africa was transparent. He saw Africa as part of his whole 'new frontier' design. There are 479 references to Africa in the index to President Kennedy's 1960 campaign speeches. In his three years in office, he invited twentysix African presidents and prime ministers to the White House – an average of one every six weeks. In contrast, at the time of the southern African crisis in the fall of 1970, President Nixon was unable to 'find time' to see Zambia's President Kenneth Kaunda, the most influential force for peace in the area: Kennedy would undoubtedly have found time to see even lesser figures, and would have tried to take a constructive lead, in spite of the thorny difficulties.

Kennedy always spoke with rare candor and without flattery to African leaders, expecting them to react as working politicians. His administration took a stance that was passively, unashamedly pro-African: since his time, no regime of East or West has ever achieved a similar image in Africa – although China now seems to be trying, in the Seventies, in its rigidly ideological way. In 1960, roving Ambassador W. Averell Harriman argued cogently and relatively successfully against waiting for a Communist threat before doing anything. Under Kennedy, contingency planning was at its peak.

In contrast, Nielsen and others score the earlier Eisenhower record in Africa as one of 'passivity, caution and hesitant reaction to events' (Nielsen's words). Nielsen notes that Ike placed too heavy a reliance on Europe-oriented diplomats. In fairness, it should be noted that there were, in Eisenhower's day, no Africa-oriented diplomats. The Eisenhower policy seems, in retrospect, to have been realistic in the context of the time. Its weaknesses, as Nielsen admits, did little if any lasting damage. The Eisenhower era laid the groundwork for the Kennedy phenomenon, and the Kennedy charisma was virtually to efface the lapses of the past. Kennedy did not invent Africa as a nexus for U.S. concern. By the time he took office, there was already a growing interest in the 'new' continent in Washington. His Inaugural Address reflected this. He said help to the world's poor should be given 'not because the Communists may be doing it but because it is right'. Macmillan and de Gaulle could not have feigned indifference to the African scene – but Kennedy could, had he wished, have gotten away with a continuance of the slightly aloof stance of Ike. Instead, like Mao a decade later, he deliberately chose to identify with the Third World's justified aspirations. Putting activists in key spots – Adlai Stevenson at United Nations, 'Soapy' Williams at African Affairs, Chester Bowles as Under-Secretary – was a measure of the Kennedy acceptance of the Third World challenge. To embassies in Africa he sent many career and non-career liberals such as Bill Attwood (Conakry), Ed Gullion (Léopoldville), Robinson McIlvaine (Cotonou, Conakry), Ed Korry (Addis Ababa) or Phil Kaiser (Dakar). 'Soapy' made 'Africa for the Africans' the credo of an Administration – although it was originally a phrase inaccurately attributed to him by a Nairobi paper: his information advisors urged him to stick with it, and he did. (Four years earlier, routine 'regrets' about the Sharpeville massacre in South Africa by Lincoln White, the State Department spokesman, had been mistakenly interpreted by *The New York Times* as implying condemnation of Pretoria. On this occasion, too, public relations advice overruled White's intention of issuing a correction toning down the apparent U.S. attitude.)

African independence, and popular interest in the 'new continent' generally, brought a fresh appreciation by Americans of Africa's limited but interesting contribution to the world at large – and to the United States in particular. There was a curious new awareness, for instance, in the Kennedy years, of the influence of such things as African linguistics and cooking on the American equivalents. Notice was focused once more on the role of African dance and music – although original jazz seems to have owed as much to Western military marches as to

Africa. The influence of African religion on fundamentalist American religious groups, both white and black, was no longer something to be hidden. There was renewed emphasis on African elements in the plastic arts in Europe and America. Researchers began looking at other possible African influences in American life. This helped humanize a national policy approach in a way that, until then, had been reserved for the affairs of Europe.

All this concern with African cultural roots for America – and not exclusively for black America – set the background for a decidedly greater commitment to African affairs, even if some of the roots, on closer examination, turned out to be scarcely credible, or unimportant. The U.S. commitment to Africa reflected, in part, a guilt complex over Negro Americans which tended to spill over to Africa. But whereas black Americans reacted by justifiably seeking to exploit America's guilt feelings, to obtain a redress of grievances, no such reaction was possible in Africa. Africa, by and large, did not suffer in any direct way from the prejudice problem in the United States. Nor had the ancestors of contemporary Africans been victims of America's slave trade – some of their ancestors had been co-conspirators in that trade with the ancestors of contemporary white Americans.

In March, 1961, the U.S. backed an Afro-Asian resolution in the Security Council asking Portugal to introduce urgent reforms in Angola in preparation for independence, following the outbreak of conflict there. The motion failed 5–2–6, but as Nielsen puts it: 'The American action rang out like a pistol shot'. The present writer was in Angola at the time, and Portuguese official anti-American fury was everywhere in evidence. The motion passed in the General Assembly. The President's brother, Robert F. Kennedy, consulted with Eduardo Mondlane, leader of the future Mozambican resistance movement. Ambassadors were authorized to talk to other resistance leaders from Portuguese Africa: meetings with envoys which had formerly only taken place in the private homes of correspondents and others now took place openly at diplomatic cocktail parties.

In the Congo, the U.S. backed the center-left government of Cyrille Adoula, despite the inclusion of the self-proclaimed Marxist Antoine Gizenga as Vice-Premier. After a mixed report by Republican businessman Clarence Randall, Kennedy backed aid for the Volta Dam in Ghana – although he later admitted to Schlesinger that this had been a mistake. When Attwood returned from Guinea in May, 1961, to report, his request for increased aid to meet Bloc competition was at once satisfied in full. In August, however, in the General Assembly of the United Nations, the U.S. abstained from condemning France over Bizerta in order not to offend the prickly Charles de Gaulle. Kennedy was always as sensitive as a liberal in power must be to rightwing accusations of being 'soft' – but that November the U.S. voted for a U.N. resolution condemning *apartheid*, and urging all states to take action (after a clause providing for sanctions had been excluded). Kennedy banned arms for South Africa. But he pragmatically refused to break relations with South Africa, or to bar the supply of arms to a N.A.T.O. ally, Portugal. He sold some C-130 transport planes to the South African air force in return for a lease of land for a space-tracking station. Also in November, the U.S. supported the creation of a decolonization committee at United Nations, against the wishes of France and Britain. (All three countries have since withdrawn from the committee.)

The Peace Corps was created, and P.L. 480 (surplus-food aid) extended: but Kennedy had little success with aid in general. The problem of recurring aid applications to the Congress made long-term planning difficult. Everything remained on a year-to-year, hand-to-mouth basis. Congress pared a billion dollars from Kennedy's $4·9 billion aid request in 1961. African hopes, says Nielsen, began to glide to the ground on the harsh realities of 'the cold war, conservatism and cost'. Policy became one of 'straddling the fence, with an ear to the ground and a finger in the dike'. But Kennedy's personal influence remained great enough for Guinea and Algeria to deny refueling facilities to Soviet aircraft during the Cuba crisis – even at airfields that were Soviet-financed.

In 1962, Congress cut $0.9 billion from a $4.8 billion aid request. Kennedy chose General Lucius Clay to head a committee reviewing aid. The selection of a conservative was intentional, but the President had expected a more objective and reasoned result. The Clay Committee rarely met, but produced a report reflecting largely the chairman's views: this weakened the Administration's position on aid even further. The report stressed the non-strategic quality of Africa.

But U.S.-centered educational aid proceeded apace. The Institute of International Education in New York handled thousands of African students. In 1961, the Project for Assistance to Kenyan Students was set up and brought about a remarkable 'student airlift' which soon seemed to 'pay off', both culturally and diplomatically. Other scholarship programs were organized by the African American Institute (A.A.I.), U.N.E.S.C.O., the Southern Africa Scholarship Program, private foundations and individual philanthropists. A.F.G.R.A.D. provided matching funds for those of a candidate's home government, for postgraduate studies. Particularly unfortunate cases like students from Algeria or Angola got special financial handling. A.I.D. educational money for studies in America went mostly to the African Scholarship Program of American Universities (A.S.P.A.U.), to the A.A.I. and to A.F.G.R.A.D. Army and eventually police training was offered under different scholarship programs: by 1972, well over two hundred African police officers had attended the International Police Academy in Washington, D.C. alone.

Although the Clay Report of 1962 had hit out at most forms of aid, military assistance had been less challenged. That year, the Pentagon came to the defense of the Azores base – although Defense Secretary Robert McNamara was not entirely convinced that the Atlantic landing strip was still essential. Kennedy went easy on Portugal that year, more in fear of drawing Republican criticism if the Azores base was lost than out of concern for the base itself. Once again, the Bureau of African Affairs and the Pentagon tangled over a N.A.T.O. issue. When it came to the Moroccan base at Qenitra, the African Bureau and the Pentagon were on the same side – but Congress was less convinced, in this case, of the base's necessity. (Qenitra is a back-up facility for the N.A.T.O. base at Rota, Spain.)

The Kennedy era was marked by frequent disagreements between 'Europe' and 'Africa' at State. Old-time F.S.O's, often with Republican support, frequently opposed Assistant Secretary Williams. The Department's officials concerned with N.A.T.O., and Pentagon officials, even opposed South Africa being declared a threat to peace – because of the U.S. space-tracking station outside Johannesburg, and the consequent 'need' not to offend Pretoria. The new Africa-oriented F.S.O's complained that Europe-oriented officers were once again, as a generation before, leaning toward a 'Munich' because the South African government was itself unprepared to appease anybody.

A high point came for the Kennedy–Williams policy when Katangese secession was broken in January, 1963, with U.S.-backed U.N. troops. On Gullion's advice, Kennedy had been prepared to throw in tactical aircraft if the U.N. offensive had bogged down. In May came the creation of the O.A.U. and Kennedy bowed to its wishes over South African arms. The contract for the C-130s was completed, but contracts for torpedoes and air-to-air missiles were cancelled. However, the 1963 aid bill was held up in the wake of the Clay Report: it was only finally passed – with much other Kennedy legislation – after the President had been slain.

The Kennedy period saw the first African military coups, beginning with the all-important mutiny in the Congo, which set the pattern, and the assassination of President Sylvanus Olympio in Togo by mercenaries from the French army in Algeria. Kennedy's era saw the repression in South Africa grow noticeably worse. In Portugal, the Methuselan figure of Salazar stiffened his position. These were reminders of the limits of the power of America, however rich and well-intentioned it might be.

Perhaps Kennedy's greatest African success was the Peace Corps. Those who initially opposed it, including the present writer, did so in the belief that it would be an invitation to the ideologically disciplined youth of Communist countries to follow suit and bring the Cold War more surely into Africa. Communist youth, it was feared, might withstand the rigors of Africa better then well-fed individualists. We were totally wrong. Totalitarian countries, it soon turned out, were unable to risk sending their youth abroad in such quantities so far from commissar control. When China did send Chinese in large numbers, in the late Sixties and early Seventies, it was under prison-camp conditions. For the most part, the Communist countries fell back on studiously unproven propaganda against the Peace Corps, thus indirectly emphasizing its success. More subtly and effectively, they asked totalitarian governments in Africa itself if freewheeling, democratic youth was what they really wanted loose in their countries. As a consequence, a few governments phased the Peace Corps out. But by and large Africa liked the Peace Corps and the sentiment was mutual. Adelaide Cromwell Hill has quoted P.C. figures to show that in the first five years of its existence, 7,944 of the Corps' 28,674 volunteers asked for African assignments: 5,981 got them.

The other notable success, although less popularly obvious, was preserving the integrality of the Congo. That this integrality might not survive the stormy decades to come is irrelevant: the political need of the time was to take sides against overt neo-colonialism. The most symbolic success of the Kennedy Africa policy was Governor Williams himself. No other wandering official foreigner has ever been so liked and trusted in Africa.

The Kennedy myth still endures, in Africa. Kennedy remains the obvious name for hospitals, schools, libraries, cultural centers built with American funds. The change of adminstrations makes no difference – just as Democratic regimes have always been obliged to honor the Republican President Lincoln. In United States embassies all over Africa, the Kennedy portrait still hangs – apparently to 'validate' the new portrait on the opposite wall.

But on analysis, the observer is impressed with how often Kennedy was forced to compromise (particularly in southern Africa) with a cautious Britain – represented by a dilettante ambassador who had become a personal friend of the President's – as well as with a fervently nationalist France opposed to African and all other nationalisms except its own, and with an unrepentently fascist Portugal. Says Nielsen: 'With . . . hindsight, it now appears that the United States might have been a better friend to Britain and would have far better served its own interests if it had recognized the deterioration of the Rhodesian situation earlier, had understood the implications, had indicated more vigorously the necessity of British action to head off the possibility of rebellion and breakaway by the white settlers, and had been prepared to strengthen the British hand by prior commitments of its own.' But the Rhodesian debacle was to occur in a slightly different era – that of President Johnson, Assistant Secretary Palmer and general disillusionment over Africa.

* * * * *

If the British were inadequate, France had proven to be a 'hostile ally' of the United States in Africa. During his 1960 journey around the vast continent, Loy Henderson went to great pains to reassure French officials that the U.S. was not coming into Africa 'in competition', merely as a friend of France. Ambassadors were instructed to stress this theme. But the French reaction in Africa, embassy despatches soon noted, was often as petty as Henderson had earlier found French (and sometimes British) attitudes to be in the Middle East. At a later period, Governor Averell Harriman also strove hard to cure French officials of their obsessive notion that the United States dreamed of inheriting some of France's 'jungle slums' in West Africa.

The issue, French specialists at State decided, was rooted in French self-doubt, a national characteristic that derived from France's unbroken string of defeats in war for two hundred years. A parallel cause and result of this was that, whereas British colonialism in Africa had originally been a notion launched by the churches and the liberals, in France the 'colonial lobby' was of the Right – hence more xenophobic and less flexible.

These factors posed problems for the West at large, and America in particular, since the inevitably critical attitude of France's allies looked suspicious to the French themselves. After independence, French Africans became aware of the minority status of the French language in the 'advanced' world: this set up enmities with the apparently more fortunate English Africans and sustained some of France's own Americanophobia among Frenchspeaking Africans.

This did not make French Africans less African. French Africa frequently voted against France in the O.A.U., and at the U.N., over southern Africa and related issues. President Pompidou's African trips were to have, on the whole, a rather poor reception. By 1970, France was on the retreat in Africa; but binding African links to Paris seemed likely to remain so long as relations between English and French Africa continued poor.

With patience and objectivity, the U.S. always encouraged African links to France – however negative for America these links turned out to be. France lobbied and pressured against links between English and French Africa – which Britain, and such French-African leaders as Léopold-Sédar Senghor, encouraged. An ultra-sensitive Washington deferred to France on this point, and declined to 'push' pan-Africanism. France's response, however, showed no especial gratitude. U.S. Embassy reports stressed how French officials consistently and actively encouraged anti-American propaganda in Africa. The principal aim seemed to be to deprive French ex-colonies of fresh aid and investment from non-French sources, particularly American ones.

The U.S. remained inhibited by an excessive fear of offending the ex-colonial powers. Even the Voice of America, despite its massive success in Africa, broadcast for less hours to that continent than the B.B.C., Radiodiffusion Française or Deutsche Welle: it was also more cautious about what it said, more sycophantic toward individual African leaders, and more anxious to avoid what Africans mostly tuned in to foreign radio to hear – political exposés and controversy.

Congo: the Gullion Embassy

Another ally with which America came into conflict in African affairs was little Belgium. The event was of course the Congo – the longest crisis of the Kennedy mandate. Hilsman says the crisis was 'like nothing else, except perhaps the croquet game in *Alice in Wonderland*, where the balls were hedgehogs and took every opportunity to unroll and creep away, and the mallets were flamingoes that interrupted every stroke by turning their heads to argue with the players'. (A *Washington Post* reporter had said earlier, in a despatch, that it was a story written by Lewis Carroll, illustrated by Charles Addams and set to music by Gilbert and Sullivan.)

The Congo posed, acutely for the first time, the problem of tripolar power. The Communist rivals exploited the Lumumba myth, which his death strengthened. There were Soviet demands for the dismissal of U.N. Secretary-General Dag Hammarskjoeld, and his replacement by a 'troika'. Most African states met in 1961 at Monrovia, and subsequently twice at Lagos, to form the Organization of African Unity at Addis Ababa in 1963; but a breakaway group formed the so-called Casablanca Bloc which harassed the others, the Congo, the U.N. and of course the United States.

Ambassador Clare Timberlake handled carefully Premier Patrice Lumumba's original request for U.S. military help, which Eisenhower, on Timberlake's and other advice, deflected toward the U.N. Through the early part of Hammarskjoeld's difficult mandate, his man in Léopoldville (now Kinshasa) was an American: Andrew Cordier. The Timberlake–Cordier period saw the famous 'battle' for Léopoldville Radio. Under-Secretary Henderson visited; Governor Averell Harriman had been there earlier. A cool, reflective Indian, Rajeshwar Dayal, replaced Cordier, to be followed by Mekki Abbas of the Sudan, then Robert Gardiner of Ghana. U.S. policy worked smoothly with all of them.

American policy was conditioned by a Cold War characteristic: the fear of Marxist imperialism. How real the danger actually was is hard to gauge: Russia's designs were real enough, but African Marxism, in the Congo more than elsewhere, bore essentially the imprint 'of Chico rather than of Karl', as one reporter noted. The irony was that what finally emerged – still under U.S. sponsorship – was a dictatorship that talked of 'one-party democracy', a concept which wags compared to that of a virgin whore.

The U.S. did not have to fight for Africa only against the Russians, the Chinese and the Belgians. In Britain, the Katanga lobby was in full cry. France crystallized its opposition to the United States in the form of opposition to the United Nations, getting its African satellites to refuse overflight rights for U.S.–U.N. planes.

There were sharp divisions in Washington also – especially over Katangese secession. The dominant feeling in the Administration concurred with Edmund Gullion, Kennedy's ambassador in Léopoldville. Katanga, if allowed to secede, would become a puppet state of Belgium. One secession would lead to another. There were economic arguments for holding the Congo together. Allowing a rightwing, foreign-supported move to succeed in Katanga – or anywhere else in Africa – would help the Communists in the long (or not so long) run. Without much difficulty, Gullion and Williams convinced Kennedy that the U.S. should be on the winning side in history. But influential Averell Harriman, who had, at State Department request, entertained the Katangese leader Moise Tshombe, in New York, before independence, had been impressed by his visitor, and opposed U.S. action against the man. Also prominently for Tshombe were retired Under-Secretary Robert Murphy and Senator Thomas J. Dodd of Connecticut – later censured by the Senate for venality. Against Tshombe in Washington were Chester Bowles, Adlai Stevenson, Under-Secretary George Ball, Assistant Secretary (for International Organizations) Harlan Cleveland and of course Williams and Fredericks.

The Congolese events helped trigger those in Angola, where a patriotic revolt began under Holden Roberto and spread to Mozambique and Portuguese Guinea. U.S. support for reform brought on the clash with Portugal and raised the issue of the Azores bases. The Portuguese protested their innocence of racism and the progressiveness of their intentions. Comments Hilsman: 'Having given three Angolans a university education, the Portuguese were now about to embark on their second five-hundred-year plan'.

Under Gardiner and Gullion – who, since the U.S. was the main funder of the U.N. operation, functioned as a proconsul – the Congolese parliament met at Lovanium University and produced the coalitional Adoula government. The U.S. had clear majority backing at U.N. (with opposition, Hilsman recalls, coming, 'permanently from France, sometimes allied with the Soviet Union, sometimes with Great Britain, sometimes both'.)

But the reduction of Katanga was far from easy. The September, 1961, U.N. operation failed. Britain refused refueling rights in Uganda for Ethiopian fighters on their way toward the Congo. French and Belgian opposition to the U.N. was vociferous. The Soviet Union, however, accused Hammarskjoeld of 'holding back'. Hammarskjoeld did agree to meet Tshombe at Ndola airfield, in Northern Rhodesia, on September 17 – a fatal mistake which cost his life. In New York, a Belgian called Michel Struelens, apparently uninhibited by scruples about the truth, was running a freewheeling Katangese Information Center with some effect. But the U.S. backed the airlift of U.N. troops to the Katanga front.

The operation dragged on inconclusively. Ambassador Gullion and Gardiner spent long sleepless nights reading field reports and drinking pints of ginger beer, a favorite of Gardiner's Jamaican wife. In December, Tshombe cabled Kennedy with an offer to negotiate. At a conference with Adoula and envoy Gullion at Kitona, Tshombe agreed to the 'indissoluble unity' of the country. But the ink on the pact was barely dry before he reneged. In the Senate, Dodd weighed in against U.S. 'bullying'. Assistant Secretary Williams and Kennedy's U.S.I.A. chief, Carl Rowan, attacked the Katanga lobby in Washington – to be rebuffed by Under-Secretary for Political Affairs George C. McGhee, who said neither speech had been 'cleared at the highest level' of the Department.

In New York, an exasperated U Thant was describing all Congolese leaders as a 'bunch of clowns'. More unsuccessful or only half-successful plans followed, with their attendant tensions and incidents. Finally, in Belgium, Foreign Minister Paul-Henri Spaak rallied to the U.N. thesis and called Tshombe a rebel. But Tshombe himself was now threatening a scorched-earth policy.

At the end of 1962, the threat implied in China's seizure of some Indian border territories led to the repatriation of some of the U.N.'s Indian troops. The Indians, including the famous Nepalese Gurkhas, had been the most effective fighters in what had become known as Rounds One and Two. But a further round of fighting was in the offing. At State, Intelligence and Research (under Hilsman) examined all the alternatives and concluded that Round Three was inevitable. The view was strongly supported by *The Washington Post*, less forcefully by *The New York Times*. The showdown approached.

An influential liberal Democrat who continued to take an opposite view was Harriman, who had a lively interest in Africa. Apart from his wartime journeys, 'Ave' Harriman had been concerned with the continent in his days as Administrator of the Marshall Plan, when he had helped coordinate mineral supplies for Europe. He had crossed swords, then, with Portuguese dictator António de Oliveira Salazar, who (he recalled later) 'wouldn't let the U.S. send engineers into Angola because they might put bad ideas into the minds of the natives'.

Harriman shared the predominant, pre-Kennedy Washington view that European predominance should remain in Africa. However, in August, 1960 – after the Democratic Convention, but before the campaign – Senator Kennedy sent Harriman to west Africa for two weeks, in preparation for appointing him to the State Department if he (Kennedy) was elected.

Harriman saw Sekou Touré in Guinea and was impressed by Félix Houphouet-Boigny in Ivory Coast and by Sir Abubakar Tafawa Balewa in Nigeria. In the Congo, Harriman dealt directly with President Joseph Kasa-Vubu, who had won out over Lumumba in the parliamentary battle for power a few days before independence. Houphouet-Boigny expressed eagerness for an 'American role' in the Ivorian economy: but he was to be frustrated by French hostility to any American help in France's favorite former colony. As part of overt measures to maintain French 'dominance', France was soon to insist on French ambassadors being deans of the diplomatic corps in all ex-French African capitals, regardless of their date of arrival.

Harriman's overview was essentially old-world and patrician: he was, for example, amused to find that both Kasa-Vubu and his enemy Lumumba were bodyguarded by Ghanaian troops under British officers. He found words of praise for Cordier; but later, in Washington, he was critical of Dayal (whom he had never met).

In Léopoldville, he told the Soviet ambassador, prophetically, that he would 'end up in trouble' because of his bid to control Congolese politics. Later, he mused that the Russian must have attributed his expulsion, a few weeks later, to machinations of Harriman's.

Cordier had grounded all aircraft, and Harriman proceeded to Brazzaville by launch, passing within viewing distance of the dreaded rapids. He asked the pilot if anyone had ever survived an engine stoppage, and got the ever-optimistic African reply: 'Not yet.'

Back in Washington, Harriman advised Kennedy to use, in speeches, the theme of Republican neglect of Africa. He advised against armed U.S. intervention in the Congo. The responsibility should remain with the U.N. He opposed the use of 'force' in Katanga.

This was the beginning, at policy level, of a long battle by the former New York governor to defend Katanga's president. As mentioned earlier, the 'commitment' had accidentally begun a few months before when Harriman entertained Tshombe – and Isaac Kalonji, later to lead secessionist Kasai as its *Mulopwe*, or priest-king – in New York.

Tshombe himself had been deeply impressed by the aristocratic reception which they received. No similar patrician in Belgium, he commented later, had ever received him so 'naturally'. Tshombe reminded Harriman that he owed his education to an American bishop.

Commenting, in 1972, on the difficulties his attitude had caused to the Kennedy Administration a decade before, Harriman said: 'I took rather a shine to Tshombe because he was so terribly pro-American and so pleased with his [1960] visit. He told me they were going to have an election [in the Congo]. He said his party had no problem in controlling Katanga, but that the Congo was not unified.' Tshombe told Harriman there was a 'wide Communist influence' in the Congo: this would put Lumumba in power. (As it happened, Lumumba was to begin his search for political salvation, after achieving the premiership, by signing a dubious contract for mineral rights with a mysterious American financier, Edgar Detweiler, and by asking President Eisenhower for what amounted to a military alliance.)

Tshombe asked Harriman for campaign funds. Harriman told him the U.S. couldn't interfere in a foreign poll, but he promised that 'we would take an interest in the country after independence'.

Harriman accepted Tshombe's simplistic, self-serving interpretation of Congolese affairs – the need for confederation, for 'more than six states', and so on. The American elder statesman recalled in 1972: 'Tshombe had a strong personality. He was not a stooge for the Belgians. He accepted, the same as anyone else, that the Belgians had behaved outrageously in the Congo.' Gullion's embassy, and most observers of the independent Congo's early history, could agree with the latter points: but in Harriman's case, it led him to support secession; he gave Ambassador Timberlake the benefit of the doubt, but later firmly opposed the policies of Gullion. Speaking a decade later, he could refer to ex-premier Cyrille Adoula as 'that stooge we put in who was supposed to represent all the Congo'.

In 1962, when Katanga was under heavy pressure, Harriman met secretly with Tshombe in Geneva. Tshombe wanted to negotiate directly with the United States and 'offered to come within fortyeight hours' if Harriman could arrange a top-level meeting. Harriman passed the message on to the State Department but 'no one took any notice,' Harriman recalls.

Harriman continued to be the strongest voice within the Kennedy team opposing U.N. action against Katanga. 'I thought the U.N. was for peace, not war,' he told the President. He reacted vigorously when U.S. aircraft were used to airlift U.N. troops in the final Katanga action, in January, 1963. But he later disclaimed any role in Tshombe's accession to the premiership at the end of 1964.

Harriman, although probably historically wrong about secession, was clearly right about Tshombe's strong, independent personality, his dedication to a Katangese nationalism that genuinely existed and was in many ways more real than Congolese nationalism. Harriman was also perspicacious, on the whole, about the poor quality of Tshombe's 'competition'. He reported Gizenga as a 'Russian stooge', which seems fair comment; he found Thomas Kanza 'duplicious', a political judgment borne out by his multiple changes of allegiance; he found Mobutu 'arrogant, opinionated, impossible,' but later revised his judgment because 'he has held the country together'.

Harriman under-estimated the dangers of Katangese secession. He apparently paid insufficient regard to the seedy foreign supporters whom Tshombe attracted, from the Union Minière and his foreign legionnaires on down – twilight characters of the sort that finally brought him to death in Algeria, a few years later. The Governor's judgment of Adoula was certainly unfair. His personal opposition to the Gullion policy failed. But shortly after Kennedy was assassinated, Harriman, while having failed to 'save' Katanga, moved incisively against Gullion, who swiftly left the Foreign Service.

The policy of 'maintaining the territorial integrity of the Congo' was almost exclusively an American achievement. The U.N. forces withered away, and Communist-financed guerrilla groups continued to sow terror and wage war on all literates in extensive rural areas. On December 20, 1962, the State Department sent an eight-man military mission to Léopoldville under Lieutenant-General Louis Truman. Other U.S. officers had already begun to assist in counter-insurgency activities and Truman's task was to make an evaluation for the future. During that month, 'Gizengists' and Katangese continued to challenge the Adoula Administration. Katangese provocative incidents multiplied, with frequent demonstrations against U.S. Consul Lewis Hoffacker's office in Elisabethville. A defenseless U.N. helicopter was shot down and its unarmed pilot beaten to death. Snipers fired on U.N. troops.

On December 28, fighting began in earnest. Tshombe fled first to Kipushi, then Kolwezi. The U.N. took the great military base of Kamina, then headed for the mining city of Jadotville: in New York, the Katanga lobby, assisted by the French and British delegations to U.N., had besieged U Thant; Under-Secretary Ralphe Bunche had ordered the Indian units in Katanga to halt their advance short of the Lufira River; but U.N. Special Representative Robert Gardiner, encouraged by envoy Gullion, delayed passing on the message – and Brigadier Noronha, in the field, held up further retransmission until his Gurkhas were across the Lufira and into Jadotville. The war was virtually over.

Bunche flew out to the Congo. Criticism of the U.N. operation had received an assist from an agency photograph showing a Belgian weeping beside the body of his wife, shot by an Ethopian U.N. sentry after the Belgian had raced through a roadblock in his Volkswagen. Propagandists rightly assumed that most Americans would side with the white civilian, not with a black soldier obeying normal instructions in a battle zone. Tshombe used the period of controversy to try to launch a new version of the Kitona talks of two years before: but this time U Thant had had enough and refused negotiations. Hilsman reveals that, at Gullion's request, President Kennedy had been prepared to send in U.S. fighter aircraft to protect the U.N. forces from air attack, if necessary. On January 16, 1963, Tshombe surrendered.

For the U.S., the successful Congo operation had been costly, and not only in terms of money. The Congolese experience was to sour the Congress on any future close identification between the U.S. and African causes. A decade later, the result – a territorially integrated Congo – remained as a major achievement; but that unity was to exist under a regime which competed in autocracy, corruption and brutality with many of those the U.S. and the U.N. had fought.

Guinea: the Attwood Embassy

Apart from Gullion, one other highly successful 'Kennedy' envoy in a difficult situation was a purely political appointee, editor Bill Attwood, who chose to go to Guinea. As noted earlier, at de Gaulle's insistence (the general used the threat of France leaving N.A.T.O.), recognition of President Sekou Touré's regime had been delayed in 1958. A U.S. mission was one of the latest to be established. An Accra-based U.S.I.S. officer, Howard Kirchwehm, had held the fort for a while – doubling as Touré's English–French translator and general advisor on diplomacy. The first U.S. ambassador, a Negro educator, had had a hard time – with the volatile, unpredictable Guinean President feeling slighted by the arrival of a 'second class citizen' as U.S. envoy.

By the time Attwood arrived in 1961, the 'Bloc' was well established. By taking repayment of its loans in goods, it had reduced Guinea's trading relations with the West – at a time when its political relations with the West were clearly tenuous. Kennedy fortunately saw, and had said, that the West's own future was 'also at stake' in the success of 'these new states and emerging peoples'. Attwood set about the uphill task of convincing the Guineans that Kennedy's America wished them well.

The earlier attitude to Guinea had been a reflection of the subservience of 'AF', at State, to 'EUR'. This subservience was, as we have seen, a natural sequel to centuries of history, but in retrospect it can probably be fairly said that it never produced a result – in U.S. diplomacy in Africa – that was not to America's disadvantage. In this case, the delay in according recognition, and the passivity of the whole Eisenhower-era policy in Guinea, created an obvious Guinean reaction to Washington. To distrust of France and Western Europe were added new, anti-American prejudices – many of which university-educated Guineans had initially imbibed from Marxist and other teachers in France.

Attwood stressed the obvious link which ex-colonial countries shared, and got many Guineans to see it too. When American envoys in Africa met in Lagos in 1961, this link was frequently emphasized. There was virtual unanimity, Attwood recalls, for recommending to the United States that a 'clear-cut position' be taken on Africa's remaining hard-core colonial situations in southern Africa. The West could not afford to be associated with the 'master racists'.

Attwood has described his mission to Conakry well in *The Reds and the Blacks*. A highpoint of Attwood's assignment was the expulsion, in December, 1961, of Soviet envoy Daniel Solod. Russian Deputy Premier Anastas Mikoyan bravely arrived the next month to open a Soviet trade fair – to be harangued in front of the diplomatic corps by Touré, who said that 'revolutions can neither be exported nor imported' and that Guinea's policies would be 'socialist only so far as this corresponds to our special conditions'. By spring of 1962, Attwood was reporting to Washington that many of Touré's lieutenants were openly pro-American and that the vitriolically anti-Western local radio had become 'blandly neutral'. Eastern Europe's fifteen hundred technicians in the country were mostly homesick, usually inefficient and dispirited. The general 'Malice in Blunderland' nature of the regime (Attwood's pun) – which added a new measure of incompetence to the nineteenth century-style bureaucratic pattern inherited from colonial times – did not help.

Attwood, in his memoirs, stresses the natural friendliness of most West Africans. 'I sometimes wondered,' he wrote later, 'if a poor white society would welcome rich black strangers as we were welcomed by the people of Guinea.' To some extent, the Guineans were reciprocating the unaffected, 'shirtsleeved' approach of Attwood's team, which contrasted vividly with the formal French and the humorless East Europeans.

Attwood, a newcomer to diplomacy, soon learned from his experience to be critical of the oddities of Foreign Service budgeting: his embassy – like all others in Africa – had only four thousand five hundred dollars to spend each year on entertaining, none of which could be used for visiting Americans, and one thousand dollars for travel (including essential visits by staffers to the nearest dentist – in neighboring Sierra Leone). In contrast, Pentagon visitors frequently flew out from Washington for 'area familiarization'. Worldwide hospitality by the U.S. diplomatic corps was supposed not to cost more than a million dollars yearly – in an age when a plane shot down in the tag end of some local Southeast Asian war could cost fifteen times as much.

. . . . .

Touré had told a Washington press conference, in 1961: 'Don't judge us by what we say, but by what we do.' As noted earlier, during the 1962 Cuba crisis, Touré refused refueling rights to Russian aircraft on the Havana run although it had been the Soviet Union that had developed Conakry Airport; this was in response to an Attwood request. After the Democratic victory in the mid-term elections that year, Touré drove himself round to Attwood's house to congratulate him, and found visiting Special Presidential Representative Chester Bowles – who shrewdly flattered Touré by asking him how the United States should handle Castro. Touré obligingly gave his opinion.

Attwood had his problems with the jealous French as much as with the competing 'Bloc'; French diplomats spread unfavorable rumors about visiting American businessmen and entertainers, and boycotted the U.S. trade fair. A French Foreign Ministry spokesman said at the time that Paris would prefer a 'Soviet Guinea' to an 'Americanized Guinea'. France feared Kennedy's promise to balance military spending with spending on a better way of saving the world from Communism – development. Kennedy declared in 1963 that 'we want to help make the world safe for diversity'.

Before Attwood left for reassignment to the U.S. delegation to United Nations, Touré could tell him: 'Every African leader guided by a conscience must recognize now the value of cooperation with the United States and [see] that American assistance is, contrary to what we were told, the most disinterested, the most effective and the most responsive to our real needs.'

The comment reflects a peak in U.S. relations with radical Africa that was soon to fade.

Relations with Nasser

U.S. relations with Egypt are a case apart. The State Department pragmatically excises Egypt from the Bureau of African Affairs; Egypt interacts essentially with the Middle

East, not Africa. However, as a frequent marriage partner in temporary 'unions' with neighboring African countries, and as a member of the O.A.U., Egypt has to be seen in an African context also.

The basic view of State Department Arabists, following the creation of the state of Israel, was that Zionist sympathies in the United States, and later the elimination of British influence in the Middle East, following the many mistakes of Anthony Eden, made a successful Western policy in the area almost impossible. The main Arabist argument for a more pro-Arab policy was that Israel had nothing to offer to the United States – in terms of oil, gas, U.N. votes, Third World support, or anything else.

The U.S. officially welcomed Nasser, a leader apparently popular enough to take unpopular decisions. The C.I.A.'s Kermit (Kim) Roosevelt had been in touch with the Free Officers' movement, through Nasser himself, since four months before the 1951 *coup*. Nasser at first welcomed what he saw as Cairo's and Washington's mutual dependence on each other. Here too, American informality was a welcome change to the stuffiness of the French and British.

As with pan-Africanism in black Africa, pan-Arabism was far exceeded by nationalism in Egypt. The Egyptians were largely apathetic and unrevolutionary. Nasser told Roosevelt that Egyptian resentment was against 'our own superior officers, other Arabs, the British and the Israelis – in that order'. But he saw possibilities for using anti-Israeli sentiments as a cement to mobilize opinion. Nasser himself, like most Egyptians, was not strictly an Arab, and had visited no Arab countries before 1952. All these facts, Copeland relates, were reported by Ambassador Jefferson Caffery, Roosevelt and Copeland himself, but doubted in Washington, although the 1952 revolution had had a good press in the United States.

Caffery dealt with General Mohamed Neguib, the initial head of the new republic, while his political officer William Lakeland dealt with Nasser, often through the noted Cairo editor Mohamed Hassanein Heykal. Neguib fulfilled the 'kindly old crook' image which, as Copeland notes, Arabs admire in politics. Secretary Dulles also sent out two Arabic-speaking junta experts, Steve Meade and James Eichelberger: the latter ghosted Zacharia Mohieddin's *Power Problems of a Revolutionary*

Government. Nasser, once in power himself, soon moved away from democratic forms toward a sort of elitist fascism; but his model seemed to be the populist Cambodian emperor, Norodom Sihanouk – or Napoleon – rather than Perón, who was the apparent model for Nasser's black African friend Kwame Nkrumah of Ghana. But like Nkrumah, Nasser began to see himself as a Messianic, indispensable father-figure. Caffery advised that strong rather than representative government was what was needed. He approved Nasser's laws against 'subversion', emphasizing in his reports that 'surveillance is better than terror' – but not explaining the difference. Paul Lineborger, a U.S. expert in disinformation techniques, was loaned to Nasser, along with ex-Nazi General Wilhelm Farmbacher and Colonel Otto Skorzeny, the dashing S.S. officer who had rescued Mussolini from the *partigiani* in World War Two.

The Nasser regime was less successful with the Press. By disfavoring critical correspondents, it gave them leave to be more critical. The Nazi presence did not help. U.S.–Egyptian relations cooled, however, over U.S. hesitations to supply real military assistance; but Nasser went along for a while with a plan for cooperation between Israel and its Islamic neighbors to develop the Jordan River. A C.I.A. operative has called the project 'a third rate idea with at least a second rate chance of success because it had a first rate negotiator, [ambassador at large] Eric Johnston.'

Poverty limited Nasser's freedom to maneuver. Attempts to achieve agreement on the nationalized Suez Canal, in 1954, or to get Egypt into what became the Baghdad Pact failed. A new ambassador, thirtynine-year-old Hank Byroade, had more success with Nasser at first, but failed to prevent the Egyptian pact with Moscow. Roosevelt suggested that Nasser use the military power that this pact gave him to make a 'statesmanlike offer of peace to Israel'. Nasser agreed, but dropped Copeland's paragraph along these lines from a speech to a graduating class of air cadets after Byroade and the State Department had reacted caustically to the Russian arms deal by what amounted to an 'ultimatum'. This *contretemps* only increased Nasser's popularity: he had learned, Copeland notes in his book, from the bitter experience of the Shah of Iran, President Chamoun of Lebanon, King Hussein of Jordan and the Emperor of Ethiopia that the U.S. rewards neutralism more generously than friendship. Nasser himself put it this way: 'Before becoming a moderating influence you have to become an influence.'

Although Egypt intervened energetically in African affairs in the early Sixties, and backed the 'Gizengists' with arms and recognition in the Congo, relations with the U.S. continued fair. But Washington failed to appreciate Nasser's support of 'terrorism', which was to come into its own a decade later as the secret weapon of the most un-nuclear forces in the 'game of nations'. Seen from a Western point of view, the Anglo–French–Israeli Suez operation of 1956 was an unmitigated political disaster. The Baghdad Pact was largely counter-productive. The U.S. fortunately opposed the first, but sponsored the second. U.S. intervention in Lebanon in 1958, although historically justifiable, also affected relations with Nasser, who began to lose faith in Western pragmatism and to seek a mystic approach to development. The 'Voice of the Arabs' radio took on a shrill anti-American tone.

Nasser, however, dealt honestly with oil companies and maintained friendly personal relations with Kennedy, to whom he had first written at his Inauguration – saying the letter came 'from the oldest but poorest country of the world to the president of the youngest but richest country'. But the Kennedy Administration's broad overview was that Nasser's actions were inimical, if inevitable. The U.S. must either change the circumstances in which he evolved, change its own interests, replace Nasser with someone more amenable or deal with Nasser as an enemy. After Kennedy, U.S. relations with Nasser were to become progressively shabbier.

PART FIVE
1963–1973
The Era of Disillusionment

The Togo Watershed: A President Shot in the Embassy Yard

When Leon B. Poullada had called on Kennedy before going out to his new post as Ambassador to Togo in 1961, the President had emphasized the importance he placed on U.S. relations with President Sylvanus Olympio, and 'the meaning this will have for the United States in its relations with Africa as a whole'. Olympio had visited Kennedy shortly after his Inauguration. Kennedy told Poullada he had been impressed with Olympio's judgment, dignity and obvious prestige among African leaders.

Olympio, by forcing France, in 1958, to agree to give independence to his U.N. mandate territory in 1960, had virtually obliged de Gaulle to hold a referendum throughout French Africa. The referendum had led to independence in Guinea that year, and in the rest of French Africa (except Jibuti, Réunion and the Comoros) in 1960.

But despite the enormous political reverse he inflicted on de Gaulle, Olympio was no radical revolutionary. Like Kenya's Jomo Kenyatta, he was an old-fashioned patriot. He was also a successful 'western' businessman. Despite his base – a poor, insignificant country – he had an enormous 'moderating' influence in Africa. This was the importance for 'United States' relations with Africa as a whole' which Kennedy had stressed in describing Poullada's assignment.

Freedom for French Africa quickened the patriotic pulse in Algeria. This led to independence there in 1962, after eight years of costly war, four of them under de Gaulle – who had come to power on a promise to keep Algeria French. One result of this second de Gaulle defeat was that France reduced its armed forces, returning thousands of its black soldiers to their homelands in Africa. Over six hundred went back to Togo.

Strictly speaking, France had not been allowed to recruit in Togo and Kamerun, its U.N. trust territories: but the Togolese had joined the French army in Dahomey, 'no questions asked'. They could, however, not draw French Dahomeyan pensions. A hard core of these veterans asked that Togo's 250-man field force be doubled to accommodate them.

Olympio knew his 'forces' could not protect him from a Ghanaian threat – virtually the little country's only defense contingency, in Nkrumah's time. Increasing his army to five or six hundred men would merely cost money which Togo could not afford, while not increasing security. Olympio told Poullada that the French Army veterans were France's financial responsibility, not his; in the Togolese army, they would only be troublemakers.

The veterans, mostly from North Togo's Kabre tribe, continued to press their cause. They began plotting with Nkrumah. They sounded out dissidents from Northern Togo in the field force. They won over the French major who was Togo's military advisor; but, Ambassador Poullada reported to Washington, the French military assistance group also encouraged Olympio to resist the veterans' demands – thus apparently engineering a head-on clash – and suggested only a field force increase of one hundred men, to eliminate dependence on certain civilian services. The veterans heard of this and went to see Olympio again. He told them that their mercenary background in Algeria would disqualify them from consideration for recruitment, even if a hundred more soldiers were taken on.

The following day – January 13, 1963 – a score of veterans, virtually all from the Kabre tribe around Lama Kara, led by ex-corporal Etienne Eyadema (who later ousted ex-sergeant major Emmanuel Bodjollé to become President), surrounded the President's seaside home shortly after midnight and staged a *coup* which ignited a chain of *coups* across Africa. The French advisers had been locked up – by pre-arrangement, intelligence reports suggested.

Olympio's lightly guarded house stood next to the U.S. chancery. The rebels ringed the block, overpowered the two guards, and hammered brashly on the door. Olympio, reading in a downstairs room, apparently guessed that some sort of *attentat* was afoot and hurried through a window and over the garden wall. He hid in an unlocked Embassy sedan.

At four a.m., French Ambassador Henri Mazoyer called Poullada to relay the news about the *coup*. Mazoyer had been contacted by the French officers, who had been released. Poullada put the flags on his car, alerted his D.C.M. Bill Hussey to take over if 'anything happens' and drove off to the chancery. He was stopped and searched by the gunmen, who ordered him to lie on the ground. Poullada argued his way out of this situation and into the building by talking about P.L. 480 grain aid to the Kabre. He managed to get the rebels out of the embassy by explaining that the building was U.S. territory. He then checked filing cabinets for security. Apparently nothing had been touched.

Poullada did not know Olympio was in the embassy yard, or that the rebels were looking for him. The frightened envoy checked that no embassy cars had been removed, but did not check the interiors, presuming that all doors were locked. The rebels, he realized afterward, probably thought that he was looking – like them – for Olympio; they held their submachine guns at the ready outside the gates. Olympio presumably thought that Poullada's footsteps were those of rebels and failed to reveal himself.

Poullada left the chancery for Hussey's house just before dawn, to prepare a report for Washington and to work out a strategy for securing Olympio's release: both men assumed that, since Olympio's house was in rebel hands, so was the courtly sixtyone-year-old President. Soon after daylight, Poullada and Hussey made their way back to the chancery. The rebels had gone. From the garden of Olympio's house next door came the sound of a woman keening. Poullada reported later: 'We walked around the compound [of the chancery] somewhat mystified until we found Olympio, shot and cruelly bayonetted, lying in our side driveway.'

An embassy staffer who lived across from the chancery

reported that day that he had been awakened by shots and had looked from a window. He had seen Mrs. Olympio, from an open shutter in the Olympio residence across the street, call out: 'Papa, if it's the presidency they want, give it to them!' Then he had seen Olympio, in shorts, running for his life. The shots rang out, and Eyadema had stalked forward and bayonetted the fallen body. The corporal's followers had then taken off in all directions. At a news conference later, Eyadema boasted to correspondents that he had killed Olympio. Earlier, at the scene, he had declared that he would tie the corpse behind a truck and drag the President through the city; but a neighbor rescued the remains before he could carry out the threat.

Nkrumah's 'Togolese candidate', Antoine Méatchi – clearly alerted in advance – had crossed into Togo before the dawn. In Dahomey, next door to Togo, President Hubert Maga swiftly had Togolese ex-premier Grunitzky (then living in Cotonou, the main Dahomeyan city, as a businessman) arrested. Grunitzky (an unfriendly brother-in-law of Olympio's) soon convinced Maga and other listeners – including U.S. Ambassador Robinson McIlvaine and General Christophe Soglo, Dahomey's army commander, who was later to lead a *coup* himself – of his innocence. Maga and McIlvaine then persuaded Grunitzky, a half-Kabre mulatto, to return to Lomé and try to secure the presidency – to keep the Kabre soldiery as far from power as possible and to edge out Méatchi (who later joined the Grunitsky–Bodjollé cabinet). Maga comically threatened to jail Grunitzky if he did not agree to 'go home and be president'. Grunitzky reluctantly gave in to Maga's and McIlvaine's demands.

Nigeria, assuming Ghana had backed the *coup* as part of its long-stated plan to occupy Togo, sent an army to the frontier, apparently ready to cross Dahomey. Ghana already had forces at Togo's western border. In Accra, U.S. Ambassador William Mahoney urged prudence on Nkrumah. In Lagos, Ambassador Joseph Palmer II did the same with Sir Abubakar Tafawa Balewa. Finally cool heads prevailed.

U.S. diplomats thus played a key role in helping prevent a tragedy become a bloody regional war. But the murder, and the seizure of power in a relatively sophisticated capital by a small group of determined thugs, did two things: it sparked a flood of *coups* across the continent, and gave Africa a different 'taste' in the mouth of official America. So the Congo was not, after all, an exception! Any country in Africa might prove unstable – even savage. U.S. policy in Africa was shaken for a decade to come by the murder in the Embassy yard, as dawn broke through the palms along the Afric shore that Sunday morning.

Conflict with France: the Darlington Testimony

One of many disquieting features of the *coup* against Olympio had been the role played by the French. Paris was clearly happier with the new 'gunmen' cabinet than it had been with Olympio. Olympio had humiliated the colonial authorities – and even de Gaulle himself in 1958. He had refused to be intimidated by Georges Spénale, the quarrelsome High Commissioner who served in Lomé just before independence. He had worked too long for a British company (Unilever) and had had his eldest son educated in England. He had revived the old Togolese link with Germany. He was, worst of all, 'pro-American'.

By 1963, it was abundantly clear that the U.S. faced open hostility in Africa from France: de Gaulle was convinced that Washington coveted his black satellites; French Africans who showed pro-American sentiments were sandbagged by French agents in African administrations; almost all American attempts to invest in French Africa were sabotaged, usually successfully.

French hostility to the United States could often take spectacular forms, with a tendency to ride rough-shod over diplomatic codes of conduct. In 1964, Ambassador Charles Darlington was recalled from Gabun at the request of the Léon Mba government: he was accused of being on conspiratorial terms with those who had overthrown Mba in a *coup* a few months before. (Mba had been restored by a French paradrop.) In 1970, Ambassador Anthony Marshall and five of his staff were thrown out of Madagascar, theoretically as accomplices in political uprisings against the Philibert Tsiranana regime.

American press correspondents have frequently been a target for French machinations. In 1971, Senegal expelled the present writer, ostensibly for reporting on a successful farmers' boycott and various other opposition activities timed to embarrass the regime during a visit by President Pompidou; all had been at least partially reported in the local government party paper.

In the case of Darlington, Marshall, other diplomats – and correspondents – one man, far from Africa, took the brash decisions: Jacques Foccart, Secretary-General for African Affairs in the French President's office. In contrast with the S.D.E.C.E. (France's C.I.A.), Foccart's competing network – exclusively concerned with Africa, and best known for its 'disinformation' skills – saw the United States, not China or Russia, as the main enemy. Foccart thus established himself as virtually the main enemy of United States diplomacy in Africa.

Ambassador Darlington and his wife fitted the pattern of those on whom the Foccart machine has tended most to zero in. The envoy, a Kennedy nominee from the business world, spoke good French, amassed more Gabunese than European friends, and unintentionally gave French colonials a bad name by doing gentlemanly things that they were unlikely to do themselves (such as getting up in the middle of the night to drive unknown, barefoot callers to hospital).

Marshall similarly believed he had the right to a large circle of Malagasy acquaintances; he had also offended Foccart by organizing a visit by a blue-ribbon group of U.S. businessmen. A stockbroker, he had earlier made a lecture tour of the United States to drum up import-substitution investment for Madagascar, where the regime largely ignored the possibility of importing cheap goods from nearby Asia and gave tariff preferences to expensive goods from France. (My own Foccart dossier did not fault my reporting, but noted a number of similar factors to Marshall's and Darlington's, adding up to a 'suspicious profile' – notably my choice of Dakar over Nairobi as a base.)

Foccart, a jowly figure vaguely resembling the late actor Sydney Greenstreet, rose to his post in black African affairs after running French intelligence in Algeria during the warfare there, and despite scandal stories in the French press of the handling of women captives by his men. One senior U.S. ambassador in Africa, Sheldon Vance, has described the experience of speaking five minutes alone with Foccart as being like 'an hour in a snake pit'.

The Foccart machine took over the McCarthy techniques: evidence against the Darlingtons, for instance, included the finding of 'American cigarettes' on some arrested politicians. Marshall, it was noted, had received Madagascar's vice-president the day before the man tried a *coup* (he had called on most of the other leading envoys that day, also – including France's). American correspondents, of course, were characterized as agents of the C.I.A., just as McCarthy's victims had all been 'Communists'.

Fortunately for diplomats assigned to French Africa, Ambassador Darlington wrote a very entertaining book about his experiences, *African Betrayal*, which became recommended reading for any Foreign Service Officer posted to the 'Foccart zone'.

From the moment Darlington arrived in Libreville, in 1961, he sensed trouble. Like Ambassador Gullion, who gave similar Senate testimony, Darlington realized that 'an American ambassador's work in these new African nations differs considerably from his life in the more developed countries. He cannot be a detached observer. If he is doing his job properly, he will soon find himself deeply engaged.' He also quotes Foreign Affairs Manual Circular 358 of September 17, 1965, as justification. This circular notes that 'traditional targets of diplomacy may not be adequate' in developing countries. In addition to 'contacts with existing leaders', officers should '[identify] the potential leaders of the future and [establish] contact with them'. Such potential leaders, Darlington noted, may be regarded by African presidents not as rivals but 'traitors'.

Darlington brought in a highly successful Peace Corps group which took some of the teaching of English out of French hands and did 'not done' things like living under African village conditions and working with their hands alongside natives, building schools. (The local European Builders Union made a protest to the Embassy.)

The envoy agreed with critics of the French franc 'zone' that French control of it was 'large and predatory'. In his book, Darlington says: 'Instead of providing these states with an allowance of foreign currencies above the amounts they . . .

153

earn, as a strong Western country might be expected to do, France takes part of their exchange earnings for the benefit of the metropole. This is the old colonial practice which is now quite rightly termed "neo-colonialism".' The practice discriminated against non-French goods. Darlington also found that 'there is little evidence that France is prepared to share the economic advantages of its private hegemony in Africa even with . . . other members of the European Economic Community'. Probing into this, Darlington uncovered evidence that the French were encouraging the corruption of ministers and top officials.

Using disinformation techniques, French officials altered or purposely mistranslated what Darlington said, or passed on non-existent messages from him to Mba. Foccart reports scored Darlington for his multiracial entertaining and his efforts to explore the country's hinterland. (Kennedy's ambassadors in Africa were under instructions to get out of the capitals, where the European bourgeoisie had set the style since colonial times, and to 'get to know the people'.)

When the *coup* against Mba foundered, some of the Provisional Government sought asylum at the U.S. Embassy. Darlington did not take them in, but sympathized that 'all these men must have been troubled by Gabun's progression toward a one-party state and arbitrary government. When peaceful means to change are denied, there is a standing invitation to resort to subterfuge and force.' (Despite substantial vote rigging, dictator Mba only got 50·38 per cent of the vote in an election after being restored.) Later, in *African Betrayal*, Darlington noted that Communist powers had not, so far, played any role in African *coups*, most of which were provoked by the rapid trend toward autocracy. Since Foccart's influence has been directed everywhere toward the creation of the one-party, non-parliamentary state, the routine wire-tapping to which U.S. ambassadors in French Africa are subject must have convinced Foccart that businessman-ambassador Darlington was dangerously radical.

In many ways, Gabun was a good 'average' place in which to study the Foccart empire: Frenchmen, Darlington reported, ran everything, from the local baker's and butcher's to the Gabunese Women's Organization and the police. President Mba's French adviser had the next office to the President's and the median wall did not reach the ceiling: the dictator could not have a conversation without Foccart's man overhearing.

When the Darlingtons accepted an invitation to visit some local schools, the Gabunese inspector who took them round was berated by a French official for doing so. When Mrs. Darlington tried to help out at a local hospital and with the women's organization, she was rebuffed by Frenchwomen. A mobile health unit given by the U.S. Navy was hardly used, although the country has one of Africa's worst health records.

As time wore on, disinformation strikes against Darlington increased. Frenchmen circulated anti-government tracts, and with them the rumor that they were printed by the U.S. Embassy. Embassy reports to State gave detailed evidence of this sort of technique. When a number of U.S. Press reports on the *coup* and its aftermath appeared in major American papers and angered Mba, Darlington was anxious to explain to Mba that neither he nor President Johnson could determine what the Press might say. Mba's French adviser kept Darlington from getting an appointment with the President.

Of the reports that apparently nettled Mba the most, Darlington wrote: 'They described some of the things that took place during the *coup*, the elections and the campaign, and they conformed essentially to my own knowledge and impressions. But they were hard-hitting and drew blood, as the truth can do. I immediately wrote to the President as nice a letter as I could, saying I regretted that our press had given him offense, but he was not mollified. I question whether the letter was allowed to reach him.' U.S. ambassadors who have served in Dakar and Abidjan, to mention only two other French-African capitals, have since reported similar experiences at the hands of Foccart's agents in presidential palaces.

Darlington thinks some of the propaganda against Americans in Gabun was locally fabricated. He goes on: 'On a different plane are the actions of the French government. What is done by calculation cannot be explained as the product of emotion . . . In [French] African countries, the [French] government has been discovered, sometimes in little scheming ways and sometimes in ways not so little, to be working against the United States, to frustrate our policies and diminish our influence.' Those Frenchmen who stood for a more reasonable policy had to pay the price: when French Ambassador François de

Quirielle threatened to withdraw the French troops brought in to save the regime, unless the regime ceased its atrocities on prisoners, Foccart had him recalled.

The thrust of Darlington's testimony was that French hostility was an important factor to be taken into account in fashioning U.S. policy in Africa. Darlington admitted that the U.S. tolerated much that it deplored in Eastern Europe, but advised that in 'the new countries of Africa . . . we should not accommodate ourselves to police states and anti-democratic methods – at least not quickly. And when the power to repress individuals and pervert democracy is supplied from outside, another dimension is added to the problem.'

That year – 1964 – the ranking francophile in the new Johnson Administration was sent to France and Africa to try to establish a working relationship with the French. To some extent, Averell Harriman found at the Quai d'Orsay, French concern at American actions in Africa was based on U.S. 'replacement' of the Belgians in the Congo (and of the French in Southeast Asia). Harriman seemed to have little difficulty convincing French officials that the Belgians had scuttled in the Congo, forcing America or some other power or powers to enter the vacuum. He left them to form their own conclusions on Viet Nam.

Harriman made a deal. U.S. ambassadors would be instructed that the U.S. recognized French precedence in ex-French Africa. In return, the French would not discourage U.S aid and investment. If signs of American 'competition' with France developed, the French could complain to Washington. (Harriman recalled in 1972 that 'they never had to'.) Paris promised to inform French envoys in the field of the terms of the Harriman arrangement. But to Harriman's disappointment, the French soon showed that they 'lacked the self-confidence' to carry out their part of the bargain, as Harriman described it later. Sniping at the United States continued, as part of French policy in Africa.

In Abidjan, President Houphouet-Boigny again told the ambassador-at-large that he was anxious to have major economic relations with nations other than France in order not to appear to be a colonial appendage still. Harriman, back in Washington, urged construction of the Kossou Dam by a U.S. firm: this was later done.

Harriman said in 1972 that he returned to the U.S. from his Johnson mission in Africa 'under no illusion about French aid [to Africa]. The French got very much repaid for all they did.' In return for price subsidies for tropical exports, they secured a captive market for goods with 'unconscionable prices'. Insistence on the French ambassador always being the dean of the corps in ex-French capitals reflected France's lack of flair in handling decolonization. France's time in Africa, Harriman decided, was running out.

Johnson and Stanleyville

Lyndon Baines Johnson came to power at the end of 1963, when John Fitzgerald Kennedy was assassinated. An immensely human president, Johnson had a deep, sincere, reformed-Southerner interest in blacks – and thus in Africa. On April 20, 1964, Johnson told an interviewer in New York that Africa's revolution was the heir to America's. He saw a danger of the world dividing on rich–poor, white–'colored' lines – 'for the wall between rich and poor is a wall of glass through which all can see.'

Although Governor Mennen Williams had led the 'dump Johnson' movement at the 1960 Democratic Convention (at which Johnson became the vice-presidential candidate), Johnson recognized Williams' achievements as Assistant Secretary of State for African Affairs, and he kept him on. But he gave Harriman a parallel appointment as the 'President's Special Representative and Advisor on African, Asian and Latin American affairs', with the rank of ambassador-at-large. Harriman toured Africa, got along well with 'Soapy' Williams and Wayne Fredericks and helped the African Affairs Bureau in its relations with Congress. He also helped organize the Congolese government's famous C.I.A.-recruited 'Cuban' air force – made up of Batista exiles. But Harriman's appointment reflected a more cautious approach to the African end of the 'new frontier' than Kennedy's or Williams'.

On June 18, 1964, the Security Council voted to set up an expert committee to study methods of pressuring South Africa. Nothing much ever came of this initiative, but the U.S vote in its favor was significant. Then, toward the end of the year, an ill-considered reaction by several African countries to a spectacular event soured the official U.S. attitude to a point where such a generously objective vote would become increasingly difficult.

The nightmare rebel regime in Stanleyville, in northeast Congo, had seized a number of mostly white hostages, including a U.S. missionary called Paul Carlson. Consular officers in the city, including a group of Americans, were virtual hostages as well. In a dramatic rescue operation, graphically described later in U.S. Consul Michael Hoyt's book, *Hostages in Stanleyville*, Belgian paratroopers arrived in American planes and brought out the victims. This operation, in which Harriman played a key planning role, virtually ended the rebel regime in Stanleyville.

The U.S. had not only saved a number of innocent lives. Washington had once again moved decisively to preserve the integrity of the Congo. The operation had the blessing of the Congo's President and father-figure, Joseph Kasa-Vubu. Although Carlson himself lost his life in the operation, a wider humanitarian need was also served: the operation prevented a fresh spate of atrocities that would have dragged the Congo's name – and Africa's – through the international mud again. Seventeen out of Africa's (then) thirtyone independent countries approved the action; but a large minority opposed it vigorously. In Nairobi, Ambassador William Attwood had to unruffle President Kenyatta, who had been trying to mediate between Stanleyville and Léopoldville when the paradrop apparently took him by surprise. At the U.N., the ultra-liberal, normally patient Ambassador Adlai Stevenson lost his temper with the critics, scoring them for their insensitive racism. Harriman concluded that 'it is better to be respected than loved'.

It was another significant watershed. A disappointed America recoiled a step further from Africa. But the Congo, at least, was grateful – and moved to expunge all memory of the various rebel regimes in 'Stan' by changing the city's name back to Kisangani.

. . . . .

Deeply involved in the tractations over Stanleyville had been William Attwood, now Johnson's ambassador in Nairobi. Attwood, who described this mission also in *The Reds and the Blacks*, found a more frankly tripolar situation in Kenya than in Guinea, with the Chinese seeking control of the liberation movements to the South – and, some feared, possibly seeking lands for Chinese settlement. The Zanzibari revolution had given the Communist powers a better foothold than in Guinea, but over a relatively small canvas; this was balanced by good-will for the West, encouraged by Britain's affirmative response to requests, in 1964, to save the governments of Tanzania, Uganda and Kenya from *coups d'état* and army mutinies. Nevertheless, there was friction between the United States Embassy and some British colonial holdovers who saw Attwood's team as 'clumsy cold warriors' (Attwood's phrase).

Soviet Ambassador Vladimir Lavrov, with several 'surfaced' K.G.B. men on his staff, faced greater problems of acceptance. By then, several East African students had returned from Eastern Europe with tales of racial discrimination there. The situation was basically simpler than in Guinea: Attwood could recall the 'non-alignment' of the United States in its early years; he could confidently advise Kenyan leaders that no aid was disinterested, and recommend that they scrutinize *all* aid offers 'the way porcupines make love – very, very care-fully'.

There was little sympathy among African governments for Christophe Gbenye and his followers when they seized Stanley-ville in 1964; there was general agreement that something had to be done urgently for the thirteen hundred (mostly European and Asian) hostages. But attitudes were complicated by Presi-dent Kasa-Vubu's current choice of a prime minister – tough, unscrupulous Moise Tshombe, who was unpopular almost everywhere in Africa except the Congo. At his appointment, earlier that year, U.S. Ambassador J. MacMurtrie Godley in Léopoldville had had difficulty 'accepting' him too. Godley had been D.C.M. to Gullion when the U.S. had been the most active national government opposed to Katangese secession. Tshombe's unreliability had become a watchword. In his secession days, a top U.N. official, Francis Nwokedi of Nigeria, had said: 'You can't buy Tshombe – only hire him for the afternoon.' Thus, Africans were cautious about how to deal with

Christophe Gbenye, since Gbenye, although a rebel, was rebelling against somebody they did not like.

In Addis Ababa and Nairobi, where Haile Selassie and Jomo Kenyatta tried to mediate with Gbenye, diplomacy was complicated by the presence of an old-fashioned Marxist, Telli Diallo, then Secretary-General of the O.A.U. Diallo favored Gbenye. Another 'joker in the pack' was Gbenye's envoy, the suave, sophisticated turncoat Thomas Kanza – who had taken the post with Gbenye after trying unsuccessfully to be appointed as Tshombe's foreign minister. Attwood describes Kanza as 'a confidence man in the great tradition of Mississippi riverboat gamblers': he was also in a more recent tradition of African cocktail-party radicals. Kanza, Attwood reported, was stirring up the tractations with blissful lies. Tshombe, for his part, angered Kenyatta by his arrogance. Kenya's Minister of State, Joe Murumbi, decided to take an O.A.U. mission to Washington, and got as far as London. While Kenyatta was considering whether to let him proceed, Murumbi took a transatlantic flight without authorization. Washington was unsure how to handle him. At Attwood's suggestion, Kenyatta made Murumbi his personal representative, not the O.A.U.'s, and he and his delegation had lunch with Secretary Rusk.

As the deadline for decision approached, in the shape of a Katangese rescue force spearheaded by foreign legionnaires, the 'Gizengists' in Stanleyville became fearful of releasing the hostages or cooperating with the Red Cross, since the hostages were their only shield. Carlson was sentenced to death as a 'spy', then held in limbo. Algerian planes had begun flying Egyptian officers and Russian weapons into Stanleyville. It was at this point that Gbenye appointed Kanza his 'foreign minister'. Speaking on radio on November 14, Gbenye declared: 'We shall make fetishes of the hearts of the Americans, and we shall dress ourselves in their skins.' Kenyatta cabled him, appealing for Carlson's life and for a 'cease-fire'.

The missionaries were not the only Americans threatened. Consul Hoyt and his small staff were imprisoned in their chancery. But Hoyt was allowed to send a message to Léopoldville appealing for a cease-fire and negotiations, and concluding: 'In case of delay, I say for myself and my compatriots goodbye.' The U.S. offered to have discussions with Gbenye. Meanwhile, to make it clear that action would be taken if the discussions failed, the U.S.A.F. flew the Belgian paratroops to Ascension Island, in the South Atlantic, where they remained on alert. In Nairobi, Diallo worked hard in the rebel interest – then requested transport back to Ethiopia in an American military aircraft. The paratroops moved to Kamina, in North Katanga, but operations were held up there to give Kanza a last chance to get a 'cease-fire' agreement from his 'government'. A paradrop was initially planned, then postponed.

With the Congolese column of Europeans and Katangese less than two hundred miles from Stanleyville, and the risk of a massacre of hostages now strong, Attwood asked Kanza if the rebels were prepared to release the prisoners. Kanza understandably said he would not discuss one issue in the conflict without the others: he wanted a cease-fire. Kenyatta found this reasonable. There was clearly no way of stopping the Congolese column, especially the dreaded legionnaires. So the operation, code-named *Dragon Rouge,* went ahead. Kenyatta was miffed, and Africa as a whole divided.

In retrospect, it would seem that everyone involved on the American side, from Johnson to Attwood, had shown exceptional concern for African sensitivity. Less than a decade before, most of the continent had been held in thrall to Europe: any hesitation to rescue European and American hostages would have been unthinkable. Nor is it likely that there would have been as much hesitation to go in if the rebels holding American and European hostages had been from a 'white' country – say, secessionist Turks in Cyprus.

African reaction to the paradrop contrasted with the appeal, the same year, by Nyerere, Obote and Kenyatta to British forces – similarly airborne troops – to save them from overthrow by insurgents. Even the less discreet, unpopular French intervention in Gabun (also in 1964) had not drawn as much 'flak' as the Stanleyville operation. President Johnson commented: 'What did they think we were going to do? Let the hostages die?'

To some extent, the French operation in Gabun had set a bad corollary; and there was a problem of humiliation: five hundred Belgian soldiers had taken the city with the loss of only one man. They had saved all but twenty-seven of the hostages. Africans had long resented the image, dating from World War Two, of the terrifying 'savage' African warrior; but it was galling, after all, to find that the white Rhodesians, South

Africans and other legionnaires in Tshombe's army were a more ruthless tribe than anything the Congo could put up against them. The Communist countries understandably exploited this 'neo-colonial' invasion: there were anti-American demonstrations in Nairobi; but by then the planes and the Belgian soldiers had departed – after a second, smaller, successful para-drop to rescue other prisoners at nearby Paulis.

When a delegation of Kenyan protesters called on Ambassador Attwood in his office, it was discovered, after they had gone, that the U.S.I.S. tape-recorder had malfunctioned: but they agreed to come back from a nearby hotel and protest again, for the record. Then they borrowed books on Kennedy and Lincoln from the U.S.I.S. Library and took the crestfallen U.S.I.S. man, whose recorder had failed, out to dinner. Kenyatta's position softened, but the local radio played statements by Gbenye and Kanza and refused to play President Johnson's. (This may have partly reflected the influence of Diallo: for his eight years in office at the O.A.U., he managed to avoid conveying U.S. official greetings, each year, to O.A.U. 'summits', but always announced the greetings of Communist states.) Murumbi remained strongly anti-American. But he soon changed policies with flexible indifference: he resigned from public service and went to work for a South African tobacco firm – but not before signing an expulsion order on his comrade Kanza.

African statements, at the U.N. and elsewhere, frequently managed to shock Americans. The Congo fiasco and Olympio's assassination were not, as events, hostile to America; but the reaction of a dozen African countries to the Stanleyville rescue operation moved the 'disillusionment era' in the U.S. into a higher key. Unlike African attacks on China or Russia, African attacks on America were published in the local (American) press, and produced a popular reaction.

Attwood was more successful in other fields. He acted shrewdly in the contest between Kenyatta and his radical rival Oginga Odinga, whom the Chinese openly – and to a more discreet extent other Communist powers – helped support. Soon, there were expulsions from Kenya of Soviet and Chinese diplomats, together with Communist 'newsmen'. Oginga's bid to establish an opposition party largely foundered.

In 1965, U.S. envoys to eastern Africa met in Addis Ababa

and again recommended a firmer U.S. stand against minority rule in southern Africa. They asked Washington for greater flexibility in planning aid, and less military assistance to African governments. Poverty, disease and illiteracy – not 'Communism' – should be the main targets for attack.

The picture was not all negative. Despite the 'Stanleyville' reactions of the year before, a 1965 poll showed that fifty per cent of Kenyans thought America had done the most to help their country, against fortytwo per cent for Britain (whose aid package was in fact greater). The U.S., Attwood commented in his book, had successfully dissociated itself from France and Britain and the notion of 'Eurafrica'. Despite its disappointment with Africa, Washington was beginning to accept that the continent was fluid and volatile, not 'moderate' or 'radical', 'safe' or 'lost'. Africanists recognized that multilingual, multi-tribal Africa's failures had been less than monolingual, mono-cultural, monoreligious Latin America's. Africa had less class conflicts (at least, for the moment), less demographic problems than the other tropical continents, more saving humor. The major political challenge remaining, Attwood decided, was not ideology but poverty – and its concomitantly 'under-developed' approach to government itself.

Three months before Stanleyville, the battle of Tonkin Gulf (between U.S. and North Vietnamese ships) had persuaded Congress to give President Johnson war-making powers. This 'Tonkin Gulf Resolution', later repealed, led to U.S. forces – as opposed to 'advisors' – being committed to the Viet Nam war. The Viet Nam conflict, as Nielsen notes, began to drain American interest and attention from 'squabbling Africa'. The overthrow of Nkrumah, in February, 1966, helped Africa's image slightly; but the bloody slayings of Sir Abubakar Tafawa Balewa and others, in Nigeria the month before, had conversely helped to make it worse. Congressional interest in Africa was now minimal.

The previous November, the settler rebellion in Rhodesia had led to the U.S. backing Britain against the white insurgents. The U.S. Consulate-General had been phased down, then closed and a U.S. trade embargo put on the rebel regime in Salisbury, in conformity with a U.N. resolution which the United Kingdom had requested.

But the forward policy of the Bureau of African Affairs under Williams was now largely halted. Williams himself had lasted longer than expected, under Johnson; however, in 1966 he was replaced by the cautious Ambassador Palmer, who only tended to show 'liberal' zeal on one African issue – South Africa, a region where he had formerly counseled caution. In October that year, Arthur Goldberg, who had succeeded Stevenson at U.N., secured Administration support for a United Nations resolution saying South Africa had forfeited its right to administer the League of Nations Territory of Southwest Africa – which the U.N. was shortly to re-baptize Namibia, after the Namib Desert. The motion set up a U.N. commission, with a U.S. member, to introduce U.N. administration. The South African mandate was officially lifted, October 27.

The U.S. decision to part company with its European allies on this symbolic vote drew little African reaction. Once again, Johnson was understandably disappointed. Moscow and Peking could now, to some extent, dictate the 'public' reactions of some of the African capitals, as of course could America's other source of hostility in Africa, France. In Britain, the newly elected Conservatives were pushing a more quietly anti-American line in Africa, as part of a general policy of 'defusing' the African era of nationalism – which Washington was seen, in Europe, as misguidedly encouraging to go too far.

Aid: the Korry Report

A noted victim of American disillusionment with Africa was aid. In 1965, the aid bill had sparked a serious Senate revolt which the liberals had joined. As in France in the era of Cartierism and the Jeanneney Report, there was a call for America to spend more to solve problems at home, and less abroad. Kennedy had had his problems in this regard: Johnson's were worse.

In 1966, Johnson asked Ambassador Edward M. Korry to head a committee to study development policy and aid programs in Africa. Korry, a former reporter who had recently held the key post of envoy to Ethiopia, recommended more regionalized and multilateral aid – an idea that swiftly caught the official and Congressional imagination; but other aid powers were reluctant to follow suit. The Senate set specific limits on the number of countries that could receive bilateral U.S. loans or even technical assistance. This closed down A.I.D. programs in twentyfive African countries, in many of which a mere million dollars could often count.

The Korry Report was published in part at the time, and was one of the documents declassified in 1972 as part of research for this book. Since development is the core of contemporary U.S. policy in Africa, it was written as the key to U.S.– African relations in the late Sixties and Seventies. It is hard, therefore, to overestimate its importance. The Report notes that 'our concern with Africa has been to lay the groundwork for a future viable Western relationship commensurate with the potential of the continent, and to prevent events in Africa from complicating a search, largely conducted elsewhere, for solutions to the problems of war and peace, or from interfering with our central strategic and political preoccupations with other regions.' Development diplomacy – aid – had worked so far because of Africa's 'yearning for material advance, the general absence of the worst structural rigidities found in other regions, to [African] openness to innovation and to [Africa's] tremendous needs'. Korry added: 'No one can tell how long these advantages will work to our benefit; we must recognize that attitudes and conditions shift rapidly in Africa.'

The Report, by its muted, pragmatic, pessimistic tone, sets the scene for the era of U.S. disenchantment. Korry criticized 'scatteration' in U.S. aid. As the U.S. had no primary political or commercial African interests, the U.S. could afford to be more singleminded about long-range economic development than the former colonial powers: but 'we must recognize at the same time that the two major European donors – France and the United Kingdom – are unlikely to increase their aid to Africa and will probably reduce it in the years to come'.

Korry laid stress on agriculture. He called for a greater role for the World Bank, because of its proven competence and of the U.S. ability to influence its decisions. The U.S. should increase funds to the International Development Agency (I.D.A.). On rural development, Korry wrote: 'Africa will be primarily agricultural for as far ahead as we can see. In most of Africa, agriculture is the sector that must provide the earnings for further development . . . If there is any field in which Americans can claim a measure of expertise in developing both theory and sound practice, it is agriculture.'

In education, high and junior high school was the priority area to develop. University-graduate positions could be temporarily filled by helpers from abroad, but the bulk of the administration of African countries needed high school graduates whose replacement by expatriates would be too expensive. Peace Corps teachers could play a major role in this form of aid. Health aid, Korry said, should concentrate on population control, and debilitating and killer diseases.

Private enterprise was 'not an easy area in which to operate, and we must be careful to make clear that we are not attempting to duplicate in Africa the forms and structures of our own country'. But helping African businessmen to compete with already established European business was not an activity which Europe was likely to champion, Korry implied: it was therefore a natural for the United States. Agricultural development, Korry said, should precede industrial development. The Report also recommended help for the Press, broadcasting and other public communications media, as well as public safety programs.

Korry found 'that the U.S. role in Africa does not lend itself to the strategies which led to the Marshall Plan and the Alliance for Progress. The U.S. acting by itself cannot have significant impact on the formidable development problems in Africa'. This was obviously a response to a mandate question, but Korry offered no explanation for his findings. (The strongest argument usually used against an African Marshall Plan has been Africa's inability to match foreign efforts with its own. Another argument is that U.S. business might become so powerful as to invite expropriation – and if this took place, the American stake might be so great that the U.S. would feel obliged to intervene with force to defend it. Some observers have argued for a 'slow' Marshall Plan, spread over a half-century.)

Korry's view was that the U.S. should ask the World Bank to deal with the three main long-term infrastructural sectors of Africa – transport, communications and energy. The committee should harmonize major pre-investment surveys. Korry reported that the I.B.R.D. was opposed to a special Africa fund being created under the I.D.A., in order not to set a regional precedent and so that the Bank should not become an 'administering agent for earmarked monies.' But he recommended that the point be pushed further.

The Korry Report was the stimulus for the establishment of satellite ground stations in Africa. Korry also recommended an I.B.R.D. conference to work out an action program for a continentwide telecommunications network. The former colonial powers should cooperate – although Korry feared that the French would prefer to compete. Korry envisaged the U.S. contributing about $150 m., over five years, to a $430 m. satellite-station plan.

Korry's main practical recommendations included setting up an I.B.R.D. African Rural R & D Institute, and more pragmatic A.I.D. rural programs. An R & D Institute would establish a roster of experts with African or related ecological experience and develop an interdisciplinary approach to African farming problems.

On education, the Report recommended that the U.S. concentrate on five fields – 'programs of excellence' in selected African universities, scholarship projects (with special consideration for refugees from southern Africa), secondary education, teacher training, and technical and vocational training. African universities, the Report pointed out, could orient training to local conditions and needs; local training could diminish the brain drain caused by students going abroad and not returning.

To stimulate African private enterprise, the Report called for new A.I.D. relationships with U.S. financial institutions, a private investment finance corporation 'in due course', supplementary programs in key countries and a 'sub-regional approach'.

Korry found U.S. corporate investment in Africa had doubled between 1960 and 1964 to $1.6 billion, but was still low. (Today, investment in Libya, Nigeria and South Africa alone totals about $3 billion; although this sum is largely in minerals, the continental emphasis is less on extractive industries than in the past.) There was a clear need, Korry said, for U.S.–African cooperation in private enterprise, to provide know-how, capital and a more effective business interlocutor with governments.

'Most African governments,' the Report said frankly, 'are unable to make the innumerable decisions which in a well-run market economy are made in response to market forces. Private initiative is the indispensable complement to government efforts.' (This was, in effect, drawing attention to the point made pertinently by the French expert in West Africa, Pierre Biarnès: that socialism required an advanced administration, and that therefore, although there might well be an argument for *dirigisme* for a while in modern Africa – and elsewhere – there was no serious hope for African development outside of private enterprise.) The Korry Report called for more formal business management training and for more on-the-job training in American enterprises in Africa, 'over and above plant requirements', and therefore supported by A.I.D.

The Korry Report found seventyfive per cent of U.S. economic assistance to Africa concentrated in eight countries: Congo-Kinshasa (now Zaire), Ethiopia, Guinea, Liberia, Morocco, Nigeria, Sudan and Tunisia. The U.S. had an historic moral commitment to Liberia and a security interest in Ethiopia. Neither could morally call on a former administrative power in Europe. The Congo commitment was the sequel to the long and expensive U.S. effort to save the country from collapse after independence. Ghana had become a similar liability, following the economic disasters of the Nkrumah era. In Morocco, a major aid effort had begun when the U.S. had real bases there, and had continued because of Franco-Moroccan friction and the now well-established Moroccan preference for trans-Atlantic over trans-Mediterranean links. Friction with France also left Washington holding the role of Western benefactor in Tunisia and the role of Western competitor with the 'Bloc' in Guinea. Korry thought more emphasis was deserved by the East African Community countries, but it subsequently proved difficult to do much in Uganda or Tanzania: Kenya, however, became a fairly important recipient of U.S. aid.

By the mid-sixties, the U.S. was supplying a quarter of all bilateral aid to Africa and over half of all multilateral assistance. The Korry Report called for a ten per cent increase in annual A.I.D. appropriations for development in Africa, from the 1967 level of $375 m. Korry also made a number of recommendations to ensure that U.S. response to African needs was faster and more flexible. Korry found that 'there are fiftyone statutory criteria in the Foreign Assistance Act, and the relevant appropriations act, which have to be met by almost every project loan. In addition, the loan must comply with the Battle Act and fifty–fifty shipping requirements. Finally, it must be approved by a series of procedures involving A.I.D., the Development Loan Committee, the National Advisory Council and the White House, depending to some degree on the size and purpose of the loan.' Korry recommended the appointment of a key A.I.D. officer to the Embassy in Addis Ababa, as liaison with the U.N. Economic Commission for Africa (E.C.A.) and later to the Abidjan Embassy, to perform a similar task with the African Development Bank (A.D.B.)

Noting that Africa depended principally, for technical assistance personnel, on former imperial powers and on United Nations agencies, the Report recommended that where U.S. 'operating personnel' were required, local governments should pay local-level salaries, which the U.S. Government would 'top off'. This would avoid 'marginally useful assistance and an oversupply of experts and advisors'. Israel and Yugoslavia were already making this requirement, the Report noted. The U.S. should use ex-Peace Corps volunteers more. 'They are experienced, more flexible, have less need for special privileges and are, in general, more attuned to local conditions in Africa.'

Korry asked for legislation enabling U.S. funding of the A.D.B. and 'similar sub-regional agencies'. He urged that the U.S. should be 'tactful and cooperative in its relations with the A.D.B., that the I.B.R.D. and other institutions and countries be pressed to take the same posture, that discreet support and encouragement be given to the U.N.D.P. (United Nations Development Program) in its efforts to help the A.D.B. and that we be liberal and generous in our relations with the A.D.B. when the promise inherent in its conception begins to be realized'. The Report criticized the E.C.A.'s campaign to promote regionalism as 'poorly conceived and overly ambitious' but said U.S. promises of support to the Commission in the past had not been fulfilled. Shortly after, a senior A.I.D. official, Frank Pinder, was seconded to E.C.A. to assist the Executive Secretary, Robert Gardiner of Ghana.

Korry and his associates were critical of U.N. agencies, saying 'There is unanimity among the highest officials in I.B.R.D. and U.N.E.C.A. . . . that the U.N. specialized agencies have been, for the most part, incompetent, that they lack energetic purpose, that they have tended willy-nilly to respond without proper study to all kinds of requests, and that their primary interest has been in extending their empires.' U.N.D.P. was seen 'by some as a last hope'. The U.S., as the largest donor, had a responsibility to ensure that the U.N. agencies behaved more efficiently.

The Report supported President Johnson's call for an international corps to be set up in the U.S. Public Health Service.

Korry felt strongly that 'the United States should provide the impetus in a major effort to create better means for sharing and disseminating technology now available in Africa, and to spur the transfer to Africa of modern technology from the developed world'. The Report said there was now a need for a continent-wide Africa Research Institute, in touch with similar bodies elsewhere, which would help determine African priorities, channel finance and set up individual institutes. 'It is recommended', the Report said, 'that this body be directed explicitly toward rural development'. The Report noted: 'If agriculture fails in Africa, Africa itself fails.'

The Report particularly recommended help for refugees from southern Africa, including aid through the O.A.U. and the E.C.A. Because Communist standards for university entrance were low, five out of six southern African refugees had been going to Communist countries for study and training. A.I.D. had already built the Kurasini International Education Center at Dar-es-Salaam and the Nkumbi International College at Mkushi, Zambia – both secondary schools, then taking between them 550 students. But this had only reduced the number of southern African students going to Communist countries to three out of four. The U.S. should continue to support these projects and invite other Western nations to do the same. Southern African political refugees should have a priority claim on U.S. scholarships to African universities. O.A.U. countries should be encouraged to employ trained southern Africans, for contracts of at least two years, and the U.S. should make a particular effort to train teachers. The O.A.U. and the E.C.A. should assist with placement; if they declined, the U.S. should appeal directly to African countries. The U.S. should pay transportation costs to the country of employment.

Finally, there was a recommendation of U.S. support for any O.A.U. initiatives to control and limit arms in Africa.

Most of the Korry Report was welcomed by U.S. Africanists, in government and outside. One recommendation, however, drew heavy criticism at the time and has drawn more since, as fears of its practical effects were borne out: this was the stress laid on a quasi-mandatory regional approach to aid.

At the onset of colonial rule, Africa had had about two thousand principalities speaking approximately six thousand languages and dialects. Imperial rule pan-Africanized the continent into about fifty territories with three main languages – English, Arabic and French – and perhaps six others of some commercial significance: Portuguese, Afrikaans, Spanish, Italian, Amharic and Somali. At independence, African countries came, on average, close to the world median in population size: since they were well above the world average in mean surface area, and below world average in administrative skills, their size created immediate problems. But many French African leaders opposed France's politically motivated thrust to break up the two great French colonial federations in Africa; in search of a single word to symbolize this policy of divide-and-rule, they fell improbably on 'balkanization'. Curiously, Korry picked up this theme.

He urged that the U.S. encourage regionalism 'rather than purely national development'. Korry spoke of 'independent micro-states' with 'illogical and largely accidental' boundaries – borrowing another myth that tribal lines were brashly ignored when colonial borders were traced. Korry said many African countries were too small or ill-endowed to 'permit economies of scale'. Basing aid on national requests would 'harden present divisions and . . . set back the course of development'. Thus, a 'regional' approach to aid was imposed on a continent still at the height of its nationalist era, and where vastness, poor communications and diversity made it frequently unworkable.

Ambassador Darlington, in *African Betrayal*, took a perhaps more prescient look at the regional issue, and one that was to win wider support in U.S. diplomatic missions in Africa. 'To state that henceforth certain high percentages of our aid must be extended through international bodies is unrealistic,' Darlington wrote. 'Such bodies mostly do not exist. Neither the O.A.U. nor the Afro-Malagasy Common Organization (O.C.A.M.) have the capability to handle aid, nor could they easily develop such a capability.' He similarly rejected the E.C.A., the East African Common Services Organization and the African Development Bank, adding pragmatically: 'As a general matter, give me bilateral aid; there is where the United States gets leverage.' (This could, of course, notably be the case in getting discrimination against U.S. imports eased or lifted.)

Darlington criticized the Foreign Assistance Act – a stepchild of the Korry Report – that limited the number of countries able to receive development grants to forty, non-development grants to eleven and development loans to ten. For no logical reason, as the ambassador to a small country was sure to notice, no small, really poor countries were on the list. The Executive Branch, Darlington decided, needed more Congressional authorization to act – something President Johnson vainly tried for.

Darlington's picture of the aid program in Africa makes Korry's more measured prose look almost naïvely idealistic. Darlington depicts well the extraordinary delays, red tape, changes in policy and dizzy changes in personnel which have characterized America's limited aid 'offensive' in Africa – along with the improbable demands for 'matching funds' from poor countries, the need for all programs to run the gamut of four Congressional committees, the loans frequently given at rates which *government* investment, by its very public-service nature, can never repay. He also recounts some 'bloopers': asked what sort of car he would like as a gift from the United States, Gabun's President Mba asked for a black convertible; the U.S. sent a white hardtop.

To the manifest regret of most locally experienced A.I.D. officials, regionalism and concentration became the guidelines of U.S. aid policy in the late Sixties. A Korry Report recommendation that was accepted said that the 'existing structure of bilateral trade missions should be further reorganized in the direction of regional administration by phasing out bilateral missions in all countries where the United States is not the major source of assistance'.

The view of Korry's critics was not that aid to the then major six U.S. aid recipients (Ethiopia, Ghana, Liberia, Morocco, Nigeria and Tunisia) should be reduced, but that the aid to others should be proportional, and should not be made dependent on policies and performances in neighbor-states, with some of which – like countries anywhere in the world – they were not always on good terms.

In fine, concentration itself was broadly seen by people on the spot as having no special merit. Key countries, it was noted, could not often be determined in advance. (Ghana, for instance, only became a politically key area when Nkrumah was overthrown and former Communist aid was rejected.) Politically and morally, Korry Report critics said, a small, successful shopwindow was probably as important as a Zaire or a Nigeria.

In retrospect, it appears that the Korry Report, which proved valid in most other respects, should have laid greater stress on the need to encourage stability through multipartitism, and on the need to stimulate what for want of a better word could be called the *khibbutz* approach – effectiveness and dedication, rather than showy developments, and particularly rather than showy failures. At the time Korry wrote, the conventional wisdom held that corruption was the greatest hurdle to African development. Today, corruption in all its aspects is still seen as significant, but the cycle unipartitism-*coup d'état*, or civil to military dictatorship, is probably now accepted as independent Africa's single greatest barrier to progress. In examining development aid as the political key to U.S. diplomacy in Africa, Ambassador Darlington probably saw the objectives and the priorities with more clarity than Ambassador Korry.

The importance of Korry's report was considerable: it became the guiding philosophy for the aid program, which became in turn the principal U.S. tool of diplomacy in Africa. But many of its better features were respected rather than obeyed.

Agriculture and rural development were emphasized, although not as much as Korry had hoped. America's immense superiority in agriculture, on which Korry had laid such stress – a point which a Texan farmer–president could be safely expected to approve – was never seriously put to the proof in Africa.

High school education was assisted more than before – although, once again, rather modestly. Valiant but usually unsuccessful attempts were made to 'marry' U.S. and African corporations in joint ventures – and reports piled up at State of vigorous opposition from entrenched French interests to this strategy. Nevertheless, first the Mid-America International Development Association (M.I.D.A.), then O.P.I.C. (the Overseas Private Investment Corporation) were encouraged.

Little, however, was done to help the 'press, broadcasting and other communications media'. Ground satellite stations certainly spread, and were a clear and substantial bonus. Co-operation with the A.D.B. and especially with the I.B.R.D. increased. Multilateralism became the votive symbol of aid policy.

But the processing of aid approvals remained virtually as slow as ever, and Congress remained reluctant to remove most procurement and other 'strings'. Little was done to expand the work of the U.S. Public Health Service overseas. The United States refused to support a cocoa price agreement and remained suspicious of all commodity conventions. Little was done for refugees in southern Africa, although this point did not entirely fade from sight.

On balance, however, the Korry Report had at least as much success as most. It concerned an area of minimal U.S. concern and was written by someone with no particular ax to grind, and with useful local experience.

Years of Doubt

By 1966, U.S. representation in Africa totaled thirtyseven Embassies, nine Consulates-General, thirteen Consulates, three Embassy branch offices and one office of a resident Consul. Plans for limited economies, by having a single Embassy accredited to more than one country, had run counter to local sensitivities; when broken relations with Mauritania were restored in 1971, a condition was that the ambassador reside in Nwakshot, not Dakar, Senegal. That year, an Embassy was created in Gaberone, Botswana; formerly, the Ambassador in South

Africa had been accredited to Botswana, Swaziland and Lesotho. By 1973, embassy offices of a subordinate type were to be found only in Banjul (Gambia), Maseru (Lesotho) and Mbabane (Swaziland); the latter two were now linked to the Embassy in Gaberone, not Pretoria. But the (sometimes uninformed) Congressional control of foreign representation funds still remained a problem to the Foreign Service. (When Guinea had become independent in 1958 – a new sovereignty not foreseen in the budget proposals the previous year – funds for a new Consulate in Marrakesh, Morocco, had to be diverted to establish an embassy in Conakry.)

Although official reaction had been muted, the liberal American public had rediscovered its interest in Africa over the Rhodesian rebellion. After Viet Nam, it produced the second largest outpouring of public letters to the Administration of any foreign policy issue – although these letters also included an organized 'write-in' by 'white Rhodesia' lobbyists on the far right. The U.S. promised special assistance to Zambia; but after a tour of Africa by Nicholas Katzenbach in May, 1967, the Johnson Administration finally limited this promised aid to an oil airlift and the building of the new, blacktop Tan-Zam Road. Harriman, then still in office, gave top priority to the road: the old rail millionaire believed the road could handle all Zambia's copper exports, thus making a railroad unnecessary to rescue Zambia from dependence on communications links through hostile southern neighbors. Zambia, Tanzania – and China – were to think otherwise. (The situation that existed – and exists – until substantial Zambian links to Dar-es-Salaam were created were roughly the same as if Yugoslavia had had to import and export goods through Russia in the time of Stalin.)

Also in 1967, the Congo's foreign legion of 'mercenaries' quarreled with its employers and seized part of Kivu province. Using American air transport, General Mobutu, the head of the Congolese junta, soon defeated them, swiftly enough to head off a 'black backlash' against white residents from developing in the Congolese capital and other urban centers.

The first shots in the Nigerian war were fired on July 7, 1967. Strong and eloquent voices were raised on both sides in this civil conflict: in the U.S., as elsewhere in the world, the

175

side-taking crossed all ideological and party lines. Some area experts also tried to counsel neutrality. Republican presidential candidate Richard Nixon spoke favorably in 1968 of Biafra's cause: but it was the pro-Lagos attitude of the·U.S. Embassy in the Nigerian capital which finally won the day. Washington, under Nixon as under Johnson, backed the military government. But the Nixon Administration tried to prevent arms sales to either side. A public statement was issued, critical of the junta for accepting Russian and Czech equipment. The U.S. gave humanitarian aid to both sides, an evenhandedness sophisticatedly accepted by Biafra, but judged intolerable by Lagos.

In Paris, President de Gaulle's African masterspy, Jacques Foccart, with some assistance from Ivorian President Félix Houphouet-Boigny, took the French government into the Biafran corner, which in turn made a pro-Lagos attitude more attractive in Washington. Harriman, who had admired Tafawa Balewa, was a staunch Lagos supporter. In counsel, he stressed the importance of Nigerian unity. By and large, Nigeria's pride in its size found a more sympathetic hearing in the United States than in Europe.

China, still caught up in its own 'cultural revolution', showed little interest in the Biafran war, but tended to back Biafra out of opposition to Moscow. Peking had problems elsewhere: in Bujumbura, the capital of Burundi, a Chinese Embassy defector was given asylum in the U.S. Embassy, and spirited out of the country unseen, following a mysterious scenario devised by Governor Harriman.

The year 1968 had opened with a tour of Africa by Vice-President Hubert Humphrey, expressing President Johnson's 'continuing interest and concern' for the continent. But by the time the Johnson Administration had run its term, a year later, disillusionment had become the spirit of the times. It was accepted on both sides of Congress that America's interests in Africa, both strategic and commercial, were minimal, at least for the time being. The Intercontinental Ballistic Missile had made Africa redundant as a Cold War launching pad, for either side, even if southern Africa could still become a site for competing launching pads for shorter-range missiles in a more limited conflict.

In his study, Nielsen noted that other crises now tended to distract attention easily from Africa. Africa policy, he reasoned, was now shaped more by American and other non-African events than by African events themselves. Kennedy had momentarily placed American idealism ahead of American self-interest, but self-interest had soon re-established itself. Policy was essentially reactive, 'pragmatic', played by ear. Except in rare cases (Tunisia, Ethiopia, the Congo), the U.S. hesitated to take a lead. Washington usually sought the impossible goal of being all things to all people.

From this uneasy period, America had however emerged with more prestige than Europe in most parts of Africa: but this was not saying much; and the signs were that American prestige, in the Seventies, was in sharp decline. One remaining positive factor was that, contrary to their irritation with France, Britain and Portugal, Africans could still find nothing 'bad' that the U.S. had done, so far, in Africa. America's sins were those of omission, not commission. Occasionally, a line of Soviet propaganda would turn up in an official speech by an African leader; Washington was naïvely expected to react by simply doing, more adequately, the good things with which the African mind associated the name of the United States – aid, the arms embargo on South Africa, investment, pressure on Portugal, and so on.

A significant anecdote illustrates this point: a Portuguese–African splinter-group leader on the Soviet payroll was given the chance to address the 1971 O.A.U. 'summit' and was urged by his paymasters to attack the United States; the resourceful fellow launched into a protest against American incursions in Cambodia; the audience was suitably startled by this strange irrelevancy – which eloquently emphasized the absence of a 'grievance' against America in Africa. This represents, for as long as it lasts, a significant advantage, which policymakers have often tended to ignore.

Continuing diplomatic conflict with France seemed inevitable, to the enduring disappointment of Harriman. But Harriman had come to African affairs less starry-eyed than most, and suffered less from the era of reverses and disillusionment. After the 1968 election, he quietly opposed the 'low profile' favored by President Nixon – as it had been favored earlier by George Ball. Harriman dubbed it 'withdrawal'. He saw the continuing need for a 'sensible aid program'. He had earlier opposed the Korry Report's insistence on aid specialization. Harriman wanted a major African role for the United States: France and Britain could each be Number One in their ex-colonies, but America should be at least Number Two everywhere. By the Seventies, even this view seemed too cautious.

Congress cut aid further in the Nixon years, partly because of lukewarm support for aid bills from the White House. Harriman commented in 1972: 'We would never have had any aid program under any Administration unless the President threw his weight behind it.' The elder statesman of African affairs also scored the ineffectiveness of the Senate Foreign Relations Committee. He found Senator J. William Fullbright, its chairman, 'two-faced' and a 'pseudo-humanitarian' who had 'even opposed I.D.A.' (the International Development Administration), adding contemptuously that 'all he does is whine'. In retrospect, Harriman also found that American firms in Africa were still too oriented toward the extractive industries, which to Africans looked like 'taking away their patrimony' – even if a few billion dollars were left behind in return. But there were few reserves of this nature in the Nixon Administration; and by 1969, already, Harriman's influence had gone; by 1972, it was even absent from Democratic policymaking. Also gone was the Harriman–Kennedy pragmatism. Even hardened bureaucrats had become infected with the paternalism common to many Africanists. Africa was now seen as a special case, politically, unrelated to the political characteristics of the 'real world'.

Friction with Arab Africa

Relations with the 'warm war' end of Africa also soured in the Johnson years. Nasser's irascibility became worse as his health worsened. Ambassador John Badeau had a difficult time. Egypt broke relations with Britain over the Rhodesian fiasco, and links with Washington became tenuous around that time: but after his African swing, Harriman succeeded in restoring some of the aid to Egypt which an angry Congress had stopped. By September 1965, Egypt was dependent on the U.S. for eighty per cent of its wheat. Institutions controlled by the United States gave Egypt $100 m. of annual aid.

Nasser took a dislike to Johnson's relaxed manners, but Zakaria Mohieddin pushed for a more conciliatory line with the United States. In October 1965, Nasser made Mohieddin premier. Mohieddin placed less stress on the Palestine issue: it was an era of 'Egypt first', encouraged by the failure of 'Nasser's Viet Nam' in Yemen. Relations with Washington promised to become at least reasonable, but Badeau seems to have failed to have exploited the Mohieddin phase. Nasser, in his search for a coherent foreign policy, was disadvantaged by the advent of multipolarity in world politics, by permanent Arab disunity, by growing Israeli belligerency or impatience, and perhaps by the Soviet commitment, which 'polarized' Egypt.

The Six-Day War, in 1967, led to Nasser breaking relations with Washington over an imagined U.S. participation. The break was essentially fictitious: the Embassy remained open with a reduced staff, under the Spanish flag. Other Arab capitals adopted the same Byzantine subterfuge. Even the Russians were not happy with developments: they had wanted a show of power, not war. The Israelis had struck before Mohieddin, in Washington at the time, could announce at United Nations that Egypt was bowing down gracefully on the Tiran Straits issue. Nasser, in the U.S. view, had allowed himself to be goaded by Jordanian taunts about bluster and cowardice. But Egypt's defeat paradoxically helped Nasser get added support from the badly frightened Egyptian people.

The Six-Day War and its aftermath were highly detrimental to U.S. interests in the Middle East, and particularly in the key African–Middle Eastern nation of Egypt. It turned restoration of friendly links with the Arab world into a major objective of policy; and it soon became clear that restored links with Egypt probably would have to precede this general restoration of harmony with Islam. Nasser presented the advantage of being a sophisticated African leader, comparable – in his comprehension of the nature of international relations – with Bourguiba, Haile Selassie, Kenyatta and Olympio. He had, like them, no exaggerated notions of his compatriots' perfection or even their perfectibility. He clearly understood that no amount of decisionmaking, policy planning or legislation would make more people more efficient. In a situation like this, if 'modernization' does not work, it is political and economic pragmatism to behave in such a way that the superpowers compete to deny you, each to the other. It was this discovery that Nasser applied in his relations with Moscow and Washington, to the principal disadvantage of Washington (his successor, Anwar as-Sadat, was to prove more coolly evenhanded.)

The U.S. was and is inhibited in its Middle East policy and notably in its dealings with Cairo, by the fact that the Mid-East crisis is also, for American Administrations, a domestic problem. Although a Jewish vote also exists in France and Britain, it is less homogenous, less organized, much less aggressively Zionist. Those who write for the serious American press are permitted to speak positively, even flatteringly, of an Arab leader or cause or country, but criticism of Israel may not go beyond the level of the tactful sigh.

The link with Israel in America is not so much cultural as electoral: most Americans would prefer to live in Beirut, say, than Tel Aviv (at least, after visits to both places, they would.) Paris and London are conscious that whereas the Arab countries can offer oil and U.N. votes, and whereas political 'friendship' with them has extensive Third World connotations, Israel can offer nothing in return for help. In Washington, awareness of this produces a permanent dichotomy in Middle East policy, for helping Israel can offer one thing in America: Jewish American votes (and campaign funds). The price is permanent difficulty with an influential Third World area, including Africa in general (most African countries have now broken links with Israel), and with the sources of some of America's present and future oil and gas.

Summing Up

In the Sixties, U.S. policy in Africa went from total involvement in the Congo to the closest that could be achieved to continental disinvolvement. Even in Ethiopia and Morocco, where the U.S. had modest strategic considerations, a phasing-out process was in evidence. There was even a reduced presence in Liberia. Development aid to Africa had not kept pace with inflation. The stress – if the very word was not too strong – was on investment, notably in Nigeria, Zaire and Kenya.

The expensive Congo fiasco, the shocking death of Olympio and the chain of *coups* that followed the *coup* in Togo, the brutal African misunderstanding of the U.S. rescue mission in Stanley-ville – all these had taken their toll of a nation and a Congress shaken by Indochina into a sympathetic reappraisal of isolationism. Africa presented an image of sempiternal squabbling, internally and with the outside world, of naïve inability to police its own problems – cholera, the massacres in Burundi, and scores of equally soluble, finite issues. Annual O.A.U. meetings had an air of unreality which tended to caution U.S. diplomacy toward Africa.

Competition with the Soviet Union, China and France also helped determine U.S. policy, but there were modest possibilities of reaching an understanding at least with Moscow. The half-serious tendency was virtually to *refuse* the challenges of these hostile powers and 'let them have Africa'. The Korry philosophy of aid prevailed, more or less, and with it an acceptance of the continuing necessity for relatively large-scale aid: but the aid policy lacked real Administration support.

Africa in the early Seventies was on the back burner of the National Security Council, and U.S. embassies in Africa lacked the sparkle of ten years before. The shirtsleeved intellectual ambassadors had mostly been replaced by more frankly consul-general types. Only the coming southern African holocaust seemed likely to shake the pattern.

Woodrow Wilson International Center for Scholars,
Washington, D.C.   1972–73.

Sources

Part One

The Moroccan, Zanzibari and other treaties are to be found in David Hunter Miller's eight-volume *Treaties and other International Acts of the United States of America* (1931). Most consular reports over twentyfive years old are on microfilm at the National Archives, where they can be traced by country of origin or, for pre-colonial Africa, by post: for instance, reports from Kasson on the African Conference of 1884–85 are classified under 'Germany', while reports from Senegal and Madagascar come under 'Gorée–Dakar' and 'Tamatave', respectively. Much material on American trade with Africa can be found in *Yankee Traders, Old Coasters and African Middlemen*, by George E. Brooks, Jr. (Boston University Press, 1970) and *New England Merchants in Africa 1802–1865*, compiled and edited by Brooks and Norman R. Bennett (Boston U. Press, 1965), which also contains the original text of the Zanzibari treaty. An invaluable source on slaving is Warren S. Howard's *American Slavers and the Federal Law* (U. of California Press, 1963). Accounts of the trials of those connected with the slavers *Catherine, Elvira* and *Ann* are to be found in the Baltimore *Sun*, December 7, 9 and 10, 1839, and April 25, 27 and 30 and May 20, 1840. Three good general studies, especially of the role of the Salem merchants, are *Americans in Black Africa up to 1865*, by Clarence C. Clendenen and Peter Duignan (Hoover, 1966) and *American Involvement in Africa 1800–1861*, an unpublished 1956 Howard doctoral dissertation by Dr. Lawrence Cabot Howard of Pittsburgh University, which concentrates on Liberia. For more detail on Liberia, there is Charles-Henri Huberich's *Political and Legislative History of Liberia* (New York, 1947). Consular matters are dealt with in an unpublished, unfinished Yale dissertation by Helen Kruse Williams on the U.S. consular service in Africa and, succinctly, in E. J. Alagoa's article in Vol. 2 (1960) of the Journal of the Historical Society of Nigeria, *A preliminary inventory of the records of the United States diplomatic and consular posts in West Africa 1856–1935*, which is also a research guide. Eric Rosenthal's *The Stars and Stripes in Africa* (Routledge, London, 1938) deals mostly with South Africa. There are massive sources of information in the historical collections of the Essex Institute and of several Massachusetts port cities as well as those of the state of Rhode Island. Belloni du Chaillu can be read in the original. Charles Chaillé-Long's two-volume work *My Life in Four Continents* (Hutchinson, London, 1912), William Wing Loring's *A Confederate Soldier in Egypt* (Dodd, Mead, 1884) and Pierre Crabites' *Americans in the Egyptian Army* (Routledge, London, 1938) are invaluable for their periods. The most accessible biography of H. M. Stanley is probably Byron Farwell's *The Man Who Presumed* (Holt, 1957). Stanley's own books are, of course, essential reading for the period. Two general histories, Robert I. Rotberg's *A Political History of Tropical Africa* (Oxford U. Press, 1963) and the present author's *Black Africa, Vol. 1* (Walker, 1967) give a broader picture of legitimate and slave trade in Atlantic Africa, the setting up of Liberia and other events of the period. Alexander de Condé's *A History of American Foreign Policy* (Scribners, 1963) gives the setting for U.S. policy in Africa and elsewhere.

Part Two

Several books just cited also deal with this later period. Additionally, for the Berlin Conference, there is Edward Younger's *John A. Kasson: politics and diplomacy from Lincoln to McKinley* (State Historical Society of Iowa, 1955). Rotberg (op. cit.) and Howe (op. cit.) also deal with the circumstances surrounding Berlin, while Volume Two of *Black Africa* deals with the conference itself and with the whole colonial period in Africa. Ambassador Sanford's papers are in the Sanford Memorial Library at Sanford, Florida, a city he founded in retirement. Consul Skinner's book on his mission to Menelik is exceptionally readable. The State Department has published *Foreign Relations of the United States* for every year from 1861 on: these volumes contain significant diplomatic despatches for each year. Some of the earlier years of this period are analyzed in Clendenen, Duignan and Collins, and consular reports are to be found in the Archives. Henry S. Villard's *Affairs at State* (Cromwell, 1965) supplies useful background for the 1930s and 1940s. To list all works consulted would be tiresome, especially for the twentieth century period. Few books have specifically examined America's relations with Africa before 1946, although there are elements of exegesis in many of the works already mentioned.

Parts Three, Four and Five

Sources for these chapters are many, especially in the magazines and newspapers of the period. Important books include Waldemar Nielsen's *The Great Powers and Africa*, Vernon McKay's *Africa and the United States*, Villard (op. cit.), Robert D. Murphy's *Diplomat Among Warriors*, Roger Hilsman's *To Move a Nation*, Miles Copeland's *The Game of Nations* and of course Alexander de Condé's already mentioned, monumental work. A perceptive dissertation is Elizabeth Mathis James' *State Department Adaptation to Independent Africa, 1952–1962*. A book dealing extensively with that particular subject is *The Overseas Americans*, by Harlan Cleveland, Gerald J. Mangone and John Clarke Adams.

The author spoke at length with a number of past and present policymakers, including Governor Averell Harriman, Loy W. Henderson, Henry S. Villard (who kindly extended me the hospitality of his residence in Gstaad), Joseph L. Satterthwaite, Cornelius Engert and the economist James Howe, to name only these. He also benefited from detailed correspondence with Governor G. Mennen Williams, Ambassadors Edward Korry and Leon Poullada, Mr. Wayne Fredericks, Mr. Taylor Ostrander of the African–American Chamber of Commerce and far more U.S. diplomats than it would be practicable to mention.

Index

Index of Ships

* Warships